Bitcoin

FROM NOVICE TO CRYPTO PRO

NAVIGATING THE BITCOIN
LANDSCAPE WITH CONFIDENCE

Felix Ryder

TABLE OF CONTENTS

INTRODUCTION

Welcome to "Bitcoin: From Novice to Crypto Pro - Navigating the Bitcoin Landscape with Confidence." We set out on a journey through the fascinating world of Bitcoin in this e-book, the ground-breaking digital currency that has swept the financial sector off its feet.

This e-book is intended to be your thorough guide, whether you're a complete novice hoping to comprehend the fundamentals of Bitcoin or an aspiring crypto pro seeking to enhance your knowledge and navigate the complexities of the Bitcoin ecosystem. By the time you're done, you'll have complete trust in your ability to interact with Bitcoin, make wise choices, and take advantage of its potential.

Bitcoin is much more than just a type of digital money. It is a transformative force that puts existing financial systems to the test and opens up new opportunities for people all around the world. Its decentralized nature distinguishes it from conventional currencies and creates a myriad of opportunities. It is protected by cutting-edge cryptography and driven by blockchain technology.

In this e-book, we'll start our journey by delving into the underlying ideas of Bitcoin. We'll examine its history, comprehend how it differs from traditional money, and explore the role that blockchain, decentralization, and cryptography play in the whole Bitcoin ecosystem.

With a strong framework in place, we'll walk you through Bitcoin's practical applications. You'll discover how to create a Bitcoin wallet, select a trustworthy exchange, and purchase your first Bitcoins securely. To help you feel at ease with transacting online, we'll demystify the process of sending and receiving Bitcoin payments.

Without talking about the fascinating procedure of Bitcoin mining and its link to the blockchain, no investigation of Bitcoin would be complete. We'll explore mining's inner workings, talk about the relevant hardware and software, and shed light on the blockchain's critical function in protecting Bitcoin transactions.

The processing of cryptocurrencies must be done with the utmost care in terms of security and privacy. We'll provide you crucial advice on how to protect your Bitcoin investments, steer clear of fraud and hacks, and strike a balance between privacy and transparency inside the Bitcoin network.

We'll delve deeper into the world of Bitcoin trading and investing as we go on. You'll learn about the volatility of Bitcoin's price, various trading methods, and long-term investment ideas. We'll give you the resources you need to manage risks wisely and stay clear of typical mistakes in the constantly shifting cryptocurrency market.

In addition, we'll discuss Bitcoin's regulatory and legal implications. We'll look at the many international regulatory environments that Bitcoin is subject to, emphasize the tax implications of Bitcoin transactions, and delve into the legal issues and controversies that Bitcoin has encountered. We'll also consider the prospects for Bitcoin regulation in the future and its potential implications for the larger financial system.

Finally, we'll discuss alternative cryptocurrencies and look at their special qualities and possibilities. We'll go beyond Bitcoin and look at the broader uses of blockchain technology while talking about the present and potential futures of the cryptocurrency industry. Finally, we'll present forecasts and scenarios for Bitcoin's future and its ability to fundamentally alter the financial sector.

By starting on this path from beginner to crypto expert, you'll acquire the information and self-assurance needed to easily navigate the

Bitcoin landscape. So, let's dive in, learn more about Bitcoin, and discover the opportunities that lie ahead for you in this exciting new digital realm.

CHAPTER
I
Understanding Bitcoin Basics

What is Bitcoin?

Bitcoin has established itself as a significant and revolutionary force in the fields of finance and technology in the modern era of digital technology. A type of decentralized digital currency is Bitcoin, that functions independently of traditional banking institutions. It was first introduced into circulation in 2009, under the pseudonym

Satoshi Nakamoto, by an unidentified person or group. Bitcoin has fundamentally altered how we think about and behave in relation to monetary systems as a result of its pioneering implementation of blockchain technology and cryptographic concepts. In this section, we will investigate the fundamental components of Bitcoin, including its concept, the technology that it is based on, and the important properties that it possesses.

A peer-to-peer digital currency called Bitcoin makes it possible for transactions to take place over the internet in a way that is both secure and decentralized. Bitcoin is not governed by any central authority such as governments or financial institutions, compared to traditional fiat money like the Euro and the US Dollar. Instead, it is run on a decentralized network of computers that is referred to as the blockchain. This network is responsible for verifying and recording transactions.

Blockchain technology, a groundbreaking concept that protects the transparency, security, and immutability of transactions, is at the heart of Bitcoin. The blockchain is a distributed database that creates a chain of blocks by storing all Bitcoin transactions in the order in which they occurred. Every block has a set of transactions contained within it, and once a block has been included in the chain, it is considered to be permanent and tamper-resistant. Because of the blockchain's decentralized nature, it is impossible for a single entity to exercise control over or make changes to the history of transactions. Copies of the ledger are stored on various computers spread out over the network.

Because Bitcoin is a decentralized digital currency, there is no longer a requirement for intermediaries such as banks to process transactions. Instead, transactions are carried out directly between participants, eliminating the need for a middleman while simultaneously cutting down on costs and delays connected with the process. Because there is no central point of failure, the network's security and resiliency have both been significantly improved as a result of the decentralization.

Bitcoin, in contrast to traditional currencies, which can be produced or created at will, has a limited supply and cannot be created more than it already exists. The total quantity of Bitcoins that will ever exist has been set at 21 million, which ensures that the cryptocurrency will always be scarce and might potentially keep its value over time. This controlled supply is accomplished through a process referred to as mining, in which people compete against one another to solve difficult mathematical puzzles in exchange for freshly produced Bitcoins.

The blockchain itself is open to public inspection, in contrast to the pseudonymous nature of Bitcoin transactions. This means that individuals are known only by the Bitcoin addresses they use rather than by any other personally identifiable information. It is possible for anybody to observe the history of transactions as well as the addresses linked with them, offering a level of transparency that is unmatched by traditional financial systems. It is important to keep in mind, on the other hand, that the level of anonymity can be compromised if the identity of the holder of a Bitcoin address is discovered by some other method.

The integrity and validity of each transaction are protected by cryptographic methods, which are used to secure Bitcoin transactions. After a transaction has been validated and uploaded to the blockchain, it is extremely difficult to cancel or undo the transaction in any way. The blockchain's decentralized structure, when combined with sophisticated encryption methods, offers a high level of security and protects against tampering and fraud.

Bitcoin also possesses a wide range of other applications, other than operating as a digital currency. It has opened the door for a wide variety of applications and use cases, including the following:

Individuals are able to bypass the traditional banking system and transfer and receive funds directly through the use of Bitcoin. This has particularly important implications for international transactions, which, in comparison to conventional techniques, can be completed in a shorter amount of time and for a lower total cost.

Some consider Bitcoin as a digital store of value, analogous to digital gold. Individuals who are looking for an alternative to traditional assets and a potential hedge against inflation may find Bitcoin to be an appealing option due to the fact that its supply is limited and it is decentralized.

The price of Bitcoin is notoriously unpredictable, which has made it appealing to investors and traders who want to profit from the cryptocurrency's price swings. Exchanges for cryptocurrencies like Bitcoin make it possible for individuals to engage in the market for cryptocurrencies by facilitating the buying and selling of Bitcoin.

Bitcoin has the ability to provide financial services to unbanked and underbanked populations, particularly in developing countries. This is especially true in countries where there is a lack of traditional banking infrastructure. It makes it possible for those who lack access to conventional banking services to send and receive money in a safe and cost-effective manner.

The way we think about and deal with money is undergoing a fundamental transition as a result of Bitcoin's introduction. Because of its decentralized character, which is made possible by blockchain technology and the underlying cryptographic concepts, it is a digital currency that is secure, transparent, and borderless. As we continue to watch the ongoing development and adoption of Bitcoin, we can anticipate that its impact on the financial industry and society at large will be revolutionary. Bitcoin has unquestionably changed the way we think about monetary systems and the opportunities that are available in the digital sphere, regardless of whether or not it ever becomes a mainstream currency or acts as a basis for more technological advancements.

Brief history of Bitcoin

Bitcoin, the revolutionary digital currency that has captivated the imagination of individuals in addition to businesses across a wide range of fields, has a fascinating background. Since its birth in 2009, Bitcoin has undergone a remarkable journey, transitioning from a notion limited to a certain market to a phenomenon that spans the entire world. In this section, we will look into the significant turning points and events that have defined the history of Bitcoin, charting its beginnings as well as its noteworthy developments, struggles, and victories.

In October 2008, a document called "Bitcoin: A Peer-to-Peer Electronic Cash System" was released as a whitepaper, marking the beginning of Bitcoin's history. The creator, who went by the pseudonym Satoshi Nakamoto, presented a plan for a digital currency that was not controlled by a single institution. This whitepaper presented the notion of blockchain, the underlying technology that would transform the way transactions are done and validated. Blockchain would allow for decentralized and distributed ledgers to record and verify transactions.

After the whitepaper was published, Satoshi Nakamoto registered the domain bitcoin.org in August 2008 and released the software's source code in January 2009. Both of these events followed the publication of the whitepaper. This made it possible for cryptocurrency enthusiasts and developers to begin experimenting with and making contributions to the developing cryptocurrency. The official launch of the Bitcoin network occurred on January 3, 2009, when Satoshi Nakamoto successfully mined the first block, which is also referred to as Genesis Block of the Bitcoin blockchain.

In the beginning, there was only a small community of people who were interested in Bitcoin. Miners joined the network and contributed computational power to validate transactions in exchange for newly minted Bitcoins. Miners also earned Bitcoins for their contributions. In May of 2010, Laszlo Hanyecz is credited for carrying out the very first transaction using Bitcoin in the real world by paying 10,000 Bitcoins for two pizzas.

A significant turning point in Bitcoin's development occurred in 2010 when the first Bitcoin exchange, Mt. Gox, opened its doors to customers. Exchanges provide outlets for buying and selling Bitcoin, which facilitated the cryptocurrency's incorporation into the larger financial system. Over the course of several years, the price of Bitcoin began to exhibit notable volatility, which was followed by a rise in discovery of new price levels.

The fact that Bitcoin was used as the principal means of payment on the Silk Road, an online marketplace where drugs and other illegal products were sold, brought attention to the cryptocurrency's connection to illegal activity. The subsequent takedown of Silk Road by law enforcement authorities showed attention on the potential regulatory problems that are related with cryptocurrency.

Mt. Gox, which had been the largest Bitcoin exchange at one point, experienced a massive breach of security in 2014, which led to the theft of about 850,000 Bitcoins. This tragedy brought to light the significance of safe storage as well as the critical requirement for comprehensive cybersecurity measures inside the Bitcoin ecosystem.

As Bitcoin gained popularity, governments and regulatory agencies around the world realized the need for legal frameworks to address concerns like as the laundering of illicit funds, fraudulent activity, and the protection of consumers. Countries such as Japan,

Switzerland, and Malta have emerged as early adopters of legislation that are favorable toward cryptocurrencies.

Traditional financial institutions and corporations started to demonstrate an interest in Bitcoin and blockchain technology as well. Bitcoin's validity and accessibility have increased as a result of major firms' decisions to begin accepting it as a means of payment. These companies include Microsoft, Expedia, and PayPal.

By submitting Bitcoin Improvement Proposals, or BIPs, members of the Bitcoin community actively contribute to the cryptocurrency's evolution. These proposals advocate for modifications and enhancements to the protocol, which would result in the introduction of novel features like the Segregated Witness (SegWit) system and the Lightning Network. Forks, which led in the emergence of alternative cryptocurrencies like the Bitcoin SV and Bitcoin Cash, have ignited debates and provided Bitcoin enthusiasts with new opportunities.

Bitcoin has gained widespread acceptance, as evidenced by the fact that there are currently millions of users of the cryptocurrency and an increasing number of retailers who accept it as a form of payment. Bitcoin has recently attracted the attention of institutional investors and corporations, who see the cryptocurrency as having the ability to serve as both a store of value and a hedge against inflation.

Scalability issues have prompted the creation of alternatives such as the Lightning Network, which allows for quicker and less expensive completion of off-chain transactions. The regulation of cryptocurrencies remains a point of contention for governments worldwide, as they seek to strike a balance between promoting innovation and lowering associated risks.

The evolution of Bitcoin serves as a powerful illustration of the revolutionary potential of decentralized technology. Bitcoin's meteoric rise from its humble beginnings as a whitepaper to its current status as a worldwide sensation has piqued the world's interest, shaken up conventional financial systems, and enthralled people everywhere. As Bitcoin continues to develop, there is a significant possibility that it may grow even further and have an even greater influence. This opens up a world of fascinating possibilities for the future of finance and beyond.

Key concepts: blockchain, decentralization, and cryptography

The blockchain, decentralization, and cryptography are the three fundamental concepts that serve as the foundations upon which innovation and disruption are built in the realm of cryptocurrencies. The combination of these factors results in the formation of the fundamental building blocks that support the transformative potential of digital currencies such as Bitcoin. In this section, we will investigate each notion in great detail, gaining an understanding of their relevance, the mechanisms underlying them, and the collective role that they play in changing traditional financial and trust structures.

In the realm of cryptocurrencies, blockchain, which is a form of distributed ledger technology, serves an essential role as the cornerstone of trust. It is a system that records transactions that is open, safe, and impossible to change. The distributed ledger, often known as the blockchain, is made up of a chain of blocks, each of which stores a collection of transactions. A chain is formed out of the blocks when they are connected to one another using cryptographic hash algorithms. This structure assures that any tampering with a prior block will render subsequent blocks invalid, hence ensuring the integrity of the entire ledger.

The applications and benefits of blockchain technology are numerous. It does away with the requirement of using intermediaries in transactions, making it easier for individuals to interact directly with one another. In addition, its openness, security, and immutability make it appropriate for use in a variety of industries, including as the administration of supply chains, banking, voting systems, and intellectual property rights.

A network or community is said to be decentralized when power, decision-making authority, and control are dispersed across the entirety of that network or community. Individuals are given more power, and their reliance on intermediaries is decreased, due to decentralization, which involves eliminating central points of control and relying instead on a peer-to-peer (P2P) network. Participants connect with one another directly in this design, which helps to build a system that is more equal and inclusive.

There are several benefits that come with decentralization. It improves security by removing centralized points of vulnerability that could be attacked. It encourages personal privacy, opposition to censorship, and resiliency in the face of setbacks. In addition to this, decentralization encourages innovation, which in turn empowers individuals in areas that have limited access to conventional forms of financial service, which in turn enables greater financial inclusion.

Within the realm of the digital, cryptography is the essential component that supports security. Encryption methods are utilized in order to ensure the confidentiality of both information and communications. Plaintext is transformed into ciphertext during the encryption process, rendering it unreadable in the absence of the correct decryption key. A pair of keys, one public and one private, is utilized in public-key cryptography. The public key is the one that is used for encryption, while the private key is the one that is kept a secret and is used for decryption.

Proof of authenticity and integrity can be obtained through the use of digital signatures, an essential component of cryptography. They make certain that the messages cannot be altered in any way or fabricated in any way. The use of cryptography is essential to the process of safeguarding blockchain networks, which it does by guarding the secrecy and integrity of transactions and laying the groundwork for secure peer-to-peer interactions.

The blockchain, decentralization, and encryption all work together in harmony to make it possible for digital transactions to be trusted, transparent, and secure. Blockchain makes use of encryption to ensure the safety of transactions, while decentralization ensures power is distributed evenly across the network, resulting in a more robust and inclusive system.

These ideas, when combined, cause traditional structures to become unstable. They redefine trust, privacy, and ownership over personal data, and they offer up new possibilities in finance, governance, supply chain management, and other areas. Individuals and communities are given the ability to deal directly with one another without the need for any intermediaries.

On the other hand, there are obstacles along the way to complete realization. Continuous development and careful study are required to address issues relating to scalability, energy usage, regulatory frameworks, and user adoption. Finding solutions to these problems will be absolutely necessary in order to release the complete potential of blockchain technology, decentralization, and cryptography.

The revolutionary potential of digital currencies is supported by three pillars: the blockchain, decentralization, and cryptography. Each of these pillars plays an important role. In a world that is becoming more interconnected, they redefine what it means to place trust in one another, encourage relationships between peers, and improve both security and privacy. The influence of these ideas as they continue to develop and find larger applications will transform old systems of finance and government, thereby ushering in a new era that is characterized by transparency, empowerment, and innovation. When these ideas are embraced and developed further, it will be possible to move closer to a future that is founded on trust, decentralization, and safe digital interactions.

How Bitcoin differs from traditional currencies

Bitcoin, a decentralized digital money, has recently emerged as a force capable of transforming the existing monetary landscape, which is controlled by fiat currencies. Its unique qualities and the technology it is built on are what have driven it to the forefront of finance industry innovation. In this section, we will investigate the primary distinctions that exist between Bitcoin and conventional currencies by analyzing their respective structures, transactional characteristics, regulatory frameworks, and potential implications for the monetary system in the future.

Transactions in Bitcoin are validated and recorded through a distributed network referred to as the blockchain. This network is decentralized and operates on the Bitcoin protocol. Because of this decentralization, there is no longer a requirement for intermediaries such as banks or central authority. Instead, there is a peer-to-peer system in place, which gives individuals more power and lessens reliance on centralized institutions.

Central banks and governments are responsible for issuing and regulating traditional currencies, which are also referred to as fiat currencies. They can take the shape of physical objects such as banknotes and coins, in addition to taking an electronic form inside the framework of the banking system. Fiat currencies are based on a centralized framework, in which central banks regulate the money supply, establish interest rates, and execute monetary policies. Fiat currencies are also known as paper currencies.

A mathematical algorithm ensures the total quantity of Bitcoins in circulation over the entire network will not exceed to 21 million at any given time. As a result of Bitcoin's fixed supply, it is a deflationary currency because the pace at which new coins are created is decreasing over time. Traditional currencies, on the other hand, do not have any limits that have been defined and can be issued or destroyed by central banks. This provides flexibility in terms of managing inflation and maintaining economic stability.

Transactions in Bitcoin are publicly recorded on a distributed ledger called the blockchain, which provides both accountability and transparency. Cryptographic addresses, on the other hand, ensure that the identities of individuals participating in transactions are kept secretly concealed in a pseudonymous state. Traditional currency transactions, on the other hand, are dependent on centralized banking systems and are therefore subject to rules such as know-your-customer and anti-money laundering laws. However, in order to combat illegal activities and protect individuals' privacy, these regulations also give financial institutions access to information regarding customer transactions.

The decentralized structure of Bitcoin makes it possible to conduct transactions across national borders, removing the requirement for intermediaries. Bypassing both banks and providers of foreign currency, international Bitcoin transfers can potentially be carried out at a lower cost and in a shorter amount of time compared to more conventional ways. Traditional currency transactions, on the other hand, typically include intermediate institutions, currency exchanges, and drawn-out settlement procedures. These traditional transactions are also subject to taxes, foreign exchange rates, and regulatory constraints.

Bitcoin's price has been renowned for being extremely volatile, with huge swings occurring over relatively short time periods. This volatility can be attributed to a variety of variables, including market speculation, advancements in regulatory frameworks, and the relative size of the Bitcoin market. On the other hand, traditional currencies are often perceived to be more stable due to the robust infrastructure and liquidity offered by established financial systems. This is the case because traditional financial systems have been around for longer. Monetary policy and direct interventions in the market are two of the tools that central banks have at their disposal for attempting to maintain stable currency values.

Because it operates outside of traditional regulatory frameworks, Bitcoin has prompted governments and regulatory organizations all over the world to ponder new concerns and face new challenges. There is a wide range of possible regulatory measures, from complete bans to the formulation of regulations that are unique to digital currency. Traditional currencies, on the other hand, are subject to comprehensive regulatory systems, which are supervised by central banks and other financial regulatory agencies.

The disruptive character of Bitcoin has significant implications for the monetary system of the future. It has the ability to make previously unbanked communities a part of the financial system and to stimulate innovation in areas other than currency use cases. The continuous conversations and research into central bank digital currencies (also known as CBDCs) point to the possibility of a convergence between the benefits of traditional currencies and those of digital assets.

The introduction of Bitcoin ushered in a new era in the history of currencies. The traditional currencies' controlled and regulated character is called into question by the cryptocurrency's decentralized structure, finite quantity, transparent operation, and capability of borderless transactions. The volatility of Bitcoin and the difficulties posed by regulations will likely remain, but the increasing acceptance of Bitcoin and the technological advancements it has spawned hint at a future in which traditional currencies and digital assets will coexist, enabling a financial ecosystem that is more inclusive, efficient, and innovative. Bitcoin and other cryptocurrencies will unquestionably play a significant role in forming the future of money as the evolution continues, and this role is likely to grow over time.

CHAPTER
II
Getting Started with Bitcoin

Setting up a Bitcoin wallet

As the use of Bitcoin and other cryptocurrencies continues to skyrocket in popularity, an increasing number of users are looking for methods to safely store and administer their digital assets. Creating a Bitcoin wallet is an important step to take before diving headfirst into the world of Bitcoin. A Bitcoin wallet is a digital repository that keeps your private keys and enables you to send, receive, and store Bitcoins. In this section, we will present an in-depth guide on how to set up a Bitcoin wallet. We will examine the many types of wallets, their features, and the security considerations associated with each form of wallet, as well as provide step-by-step directions on how to create a wallet and keep it secure.

Bitcoin wallets can either be software applications or physical devices that contain a user's private keys. These private keys are required in order to access and manage a user's Bitcoin holdings. They give you the ability to send and receive Bitcoins, keep track of your balance, and check the history of your transactions. There are a few distinct kinds of Bitcoin wallets available, and each one strikes a unique balance between the two priorities of ease of use and safety.

Desktop wallets, mobile wallets, and web-based wallets are the three primary categories under which software wallets fall. Desktop wallets are the most frequent sort of Bitcoin wallet.

Desktop wallets are applications that are downloaded and installed on your personal computer or laptop. They provide you complete control over the private keys associated with your wallet. Exodus, Electrum, and Bitcoin Core are a few examples of such software.

Because your private keys are kept locally, these wallets provide an exceptionally high level of protection for your cryptocurrency. However, in order to guarantee the protection of your Bitcoins, they need to be updated and backed up on a regular basis.

Mobile wallets make it simple to access your Bitcoins while you're on the go because they're made to work on portable devices like tablets and smartphones. In general, they are easy to use and provide heightened levels of security features. Mycelium, Breadwallet, and Trust Wallet are three well-known examples of popular mobile wallets. If the security of your smartphone is compromised, mobile wallets may be more susceptible to hacking, for this reason, it is essential to protect your device using passcodes and biometric authentication.

Web-based wallets are accessible through web browsers, and third-party service providers are responsible for their provision. They are advantageous since you can access your wallet from any device that has an internet connection. This makes them convenient. Web-based wallets, on the other hand, are more prone to being hacked and have their security compromised. Coinbase, Blockchain.info, and MyEtherWallet are a few examples of such services. To ensure the safety of your private keys while utilizing web-based wallets, it is critical to select service providers with a solid reputation, turn on two-factor authentication (2FA), and use extreme caution.

Hardware wallets are physical devices that are developed expressly for the purpose of storing private keys offline. As a result, they offer a Bitcoin storage option that is extremely safe. Because the private keys are never transferred off the device, they provide protection against malware and other internet risks. Ledger, Trezor, and Keep Key are three well-known brands that provide hardware wallets. You must connect a hardware wallet to either your computer or your mobile device before you can start a transaction while using one. The private keys are kept safely on the hardware device so that the user is protected from any attacks that may come from the internet.

Printing out both your private and public keys on a physical piece of paper is required in order to use a paper wallet. By using this method, your keys will remain offline, which will provide increased protection against hackers and other internet risks. A paper wallet can be created using websites or software programs that have been developed particularly for the purpose of creating paper wallets. However, care needs to be taken to ensure the paper wallet is kept in a secure location and is shielded from harm at all times. Paper wallets are most commonly employed for long-term storage rather than for use in frequent financial dealings.

The following procedures need to be completed in order to successfully create and protect a Bitcoin wallet:

Do in-depth research on the various types of Bitcoin wallets available, and select one that best fits your requirements and personal preferences on the level of security. It is important to think about things like the user experience, the safety features, and the track record of the wallet provider.

If you choose for a software wallet, you must download the wallet program from the wallet provider's official website. In order to avoid downloading malware or falling victim to a phishing scam, you should make sure that the file you download comes from a reliable source and check the file's integrity after it has been downloaded.

The initialization procedure for each wallet is different, but in general, it entails coming up with a secure and unique password and producing a backup seed phrase. Because it enables you to restore your wallet in the event that it becomes corrupted or lost, the backup seed phrase is an essential component. Protect yourself by writing down this seed phrase and storing it in a safe place that is not online.

You may improve the safety of your wallet by enabling two-factor authentication (also known as 2FA) if it is an option, upgrading the wallet's software on a regular basis, and ensuring that the operating system and antivirus software on your device are always up to date. Additionally, you should think about encrypting your wallet with a strong password and making use of any safety features offered by the program that manages your wallet.

It is absolutely necessary to make frequent backups of your wallet and to store them in a safe location. It is essential that this backup contains both the wallet software and the backup seed phrase. Investigate your alternatives for offline as well as cloud-based backups to guarantee redundancy and protection against loss of data. In addition, you should get some practice restoring your wallet from the backup to verify that the process is ingrained in your memory and works properly.

When creating a Bitcoin wallet, there are a few different aspects of security that need to be taken into consideration:

The most vulnerable piece of information contained in your Bitcoin wallet is your private key. Always keep them safe, and under no circumstances should you ever reveal them to anyone. For further peace of mind, you might want to consider hiding them away in an offline wallet or on a hardware wallet.

When communicating with internet sites that are related to Bitcoin wallets, proceed with extreme caution. Be wary of phishing attacks, in which dishonest individuals pretend to be legitimate wallet providers in order to gain private key information. Utilize a reliable antivirus program that is kept up to date to keep your computer safe against potentially harmful software

Maintain an awareness of any updates or security fixes that are made available by the wallet provider. Keeping the software on your wallet up to date might assist in providing protection against potential security vulnerabilities.

When joining the world of cryptocurrencies, one of the most important steps to take is to create a Bitcoin wallet. Individuals are able to make educated judgments regarding the most appropriate wallet option for their needs by first gaining an awareness of the many types of wallets, as well as the features and security considerations associated with each type. Keeping private keys safe and adhering to industry standards is of the utmost importance, regardless of whether one chooses for a software wallet due to its convenience, a hardware wallet due to its increased security, or a paper wallet due to its offline storage capabilities. Keeping the safety and honesty of your Bitcoin wallet under check during the ongoing evolution of the Bitcoin ecosystem is the best way to guarantee a Bitcoin experience that is both rewarding and risk-free.

Choosing a reputable Bitcoin exchange

Bitcoin exchanges are becoming increasingly attractive destinations for people who are interested in entering the realm of digital assets due to the continued rise in popularity of Bitcoin and other cryptocurrencies. These platforms act as middlemen, facilitating transactions including the purchase, sale, and exchange of cryptocurrency. However, because there are so many exchanges to select from, it is absolutely necessary to pick one that has a good reputation and can be relied on in order to keep your money safe and have a trading experience that goes off without any problems. In this section, we will discuss the several aspects that should be taken into account when choosing a Bitcoin exchange. Some of these aspects include safety precautions, regulatory compliance, user experience, customer service, and liquidity.

A trustworthy Bitcoin exchange places a high priority on implementing strict security measures to keep customer funds safe. This involves adhering to regulatory compliance requirements, adopting two-factor authentication (2FA), making use of cold storage for offline asset preservation, and providing insurance coverage against any losses caused by security breaches.

Transparency and adherence to legal standards can both be ensured by selecting a Bitcoin exchange that is in compliance with applicable rules and possesses the appropriate licensing. If you want to improve the safety and honesty of your trading activities, you should look for exchanges that are registered with the regulatory agencies in the jurisdictions in which they operate.

The overall trading experience is improved with a user interface that is easy to navigate. Look for exchanges that have user-friendly interfaces that make navigation easy and trading execution smooth. You should give some thought to the many trading choices that are accessible, such as spot trading, margin trading, futures contracts, and decentralized trading, in order to pick an exchange that is compatible with your trading preferences and objectives.

It is absolutely essential to have customer assistance that is both effective and quick to respond in order to address any problems, questions, or technical issues that may come up. Choose a market that has various support methods, such as email, live chat, or the phone, and do some research to find out how long it often takes for the market to respond. Consider the reputation of the marketplace, and look at the evaluations left by previous customers, to get an idea of the kind of customer service it offers.

You should check to see if the exchange supports the fiat currency you want to use for deposits and withdrawals before you sign up. Assess the availability of payment methods that are both convenient and secure, such as bank transfers, credit/debit cards, or other payment processors, in order to ensure that the process of swapping fiat currency for cryptocurrency goes off without any difficulties.

It is essential, in order to confirm the reliability of the exchange, to conduct research on its reputation and track record. To determine the legitimacy of the exchange, it is helpful to look through the user comments, news stories, and evaluations offered by reliable sources. Think about how long the exchange has been operating, as it is normally more reassuring to deal with an established platform that has been there for a while.

It is absolutely necessary to make use of a Bitcoin exchange that has a solid reputation in order to guarantee the safety of your transactions and the efficacy of your trading activities. You will be able to make an educated decision if you take into account aspects of the cryptocurrency exchange like its reputation and track record, as well as its security measures, regulatory compliance, user experience, customer support, liquidity, and support for fiat currencies. Conduct exhaustive research and exercise due diligence in order to select a trading platform that is compatible with your trading objectives, offers a safe trading environment, and protects your funds. If you choose the right exchange, you will be able to confidently navigate the world of cryptocurrencies, secure in the knowledge that your digital assets will be safeguarded and that the trading process will go off without a hitch.

Securing your Bitcoin holdings

It is absolutely necessary for Bitcoin holders to place a high priority on protecting their digital assets, given that both the value of Bitcoin and its popularity are continuing to rise. Due to the fact that Bitcoin is a decentralized digital currency, special precautions need to be taken in order to protect it from many possible threats, including theft, hacking, and loss. In this section, we will discuss a variety of approaches and best practices for preserving your Bitcoin holdings. We will discuss a variety of topics, some of which are as follows: wallet security; backup and recovery choices; offline storage methods; multisignature wallets; ongoing vigilance; and the necessity of complete security measures.

Because it is a digital currency, Bitcoin relies on cryptographic keys rather than physical assets, which presents a distinct range of difficulties in terms of maintaining its security. Users are obligated to implement preventative security measures due to the unchangeable characteristic of Bitcoin transactions as well as the possibility of their funds being lost or stolen. As a Bitcoin holder, you are the sole owner of your digital assets and the custodian of those assets. Because of this, it is your obligation to keep your Bitcoins safe and secure.

Finding a Bitcoin wallet that is trustworthy is essential if you want to keep your possessions safe. Paper wallets, hardware wallets, and software wallets all provide varying degrees of convenience and security for storing digital currency. Keeping your wallet's software updated and enabling two-factor authentication (2FA), and using strong passwords and encryption are all key security practices.

It is absolutely necessary to create backups of your Bitcoin wallet on a regular basis in order to protect against the loss of data. It is essential that backups contain not just the wallet software but also the private keys associated with each of your Bitcoin addresses. Redundancy and protection from data loss, theft, or destruction can be achieved by the use of a variety of backup strategies, such as offline storage, hardware devices, cloud-based solutions, and multiple physical copies. Get yourself familiar with the process of recovering data, and then test it out using your backups to make sure that it is both accessible and working.

An additional degree of protection can be afforded to your Bitcoin assets by using a "cold wallet" to store a sizeable percentage of those holdings offline. Offline storage methods that are becoming increasingly popular include hardware wallets and paper wallets. By storing private keys offline in a physical device, hardware wallets reduce the likelihood of being targeted by cybercriminals. To use a paper wallet, you must first print your private keys and Bitcoin addresses on paper and then store the paper wallet offline. The danger of losing all of one's holdings due to the failure of a single wallet or storage mechanism can be reduced further by splitting and diversifying those holdings over many wallets and storage methods.

Wallets that support multiple signatures, often known as multisig, provide an additional layer of protection by necessitating the use of more than one signature to validate transactions. When numerous private keys are involved, it is far more difficult for potential attackers to gain illegal access to the system. These wallets are especially helpful for big Bitcoin holdings or joint accounts since they offer greater security and protection against single points of failure.

Important ongoing security practices include performing regular security audits, updating wallet software on a consistent basis, avoiding accessing wallets while using public Wi-Fi networks, and being wary of phishing attempts and social engineering techniques. Protecting oneself against potential hazards and vulnerabilities requires keeping up to date on newly discovered dangers and adjusting one's security protocols to account for these changes.

It is absolutely necessary to prevent your Bitcoin assets from being stolen, hacked, or otherwise lost by taking the necessary precautions. You can dramatically lower the danger of security breaches by implementing strict wallet security procedures, frequently backing up your wallet, utilizing offline storage methods, investigating multisignature wallets, practicing continual vigilance, and being educated about the most recent security practices. Keep in mind that maintaining security is a continual effort that calls for agility as well as maintaining awareness of newly surfaced dangers. You will have the ability to successfully traverse the world of Bitcoin, protect your assets, and enjoy the benefits of digital wealth in a secure manner if you have the appropriate security measures in place.

Buying your first Bitcoin

People all around the world who are interested in entering the realm of cryptocurrencies have been increasingly curious about Bitcoin as both its popularity and worth have been on the rise. However, the process of purchasing Bitcoin and navigating the complicated terrain might be intimidating for those who are just starting out. In this section, we will present an in-depth guide on how to buy your first Bitcoin. This guide will cover fundamental ideas, selecting a trusted exchange or platform, explaining wallet options, assuring security, and delivering detailed instructions to assist you in making your first Bitcoin purchase.

Blockchain is the name of the underlying technology that powers the decentralized digital currency known as Bitcoin. It enables transactions between individuals directly, without the need for intermediaries such as banks in the process. By offering a decentralized alternative to the conventional banking systems that are in place, Bitcoin has the potential to bring about a huge disruption in the global financial system. It is important that you educate yourself on fundamental ideas concerning Bitcoin prior to beginning your adventure with the cryptocurrency. These fundamental ideas include blockchain technology, mining, wallets, private and public keys, and the function that exchanges play in making Bitcoin transactions possible.

In order to buy Bitcoin, you will need to select a Bitcoin exchange or platform that has a good reputation and can be trusted. Conduct exhaustive study and exercise proper diligence in order to examine the various accessible possibilities. Think about things like the safety precautions, the user experience, the costs, the nations that are supported, the customer support, and the compliance regulations. Choose cryptocurrency exchanges that place a high priority on the security of their users and have strict procedures in place to prevent against theft and hacking.

Your private keys, which are required in order to access and manage your Bitcoins, are stored in a Bitcoin wallet, which is a digital storage location. Gain an understanding of the various types of Bitcoin wallets that are now accessible, including as desktop, mobile, and web-based software wallets, hardware wallets, paper wallets, and multisignature wallets. There are varying levels of convenience, accessibility, and safety that come included with each model. Select a wallet that fulfills your requirements and caters to your tastes by paying attention to aspects such as its user-friendliness, safety features, and availability of backups.

When it comes to managing Bitcoin and guarding your digital wealth, maintaining a high level of security is of the utmost significance. To further strengthen your safety, make sure to adopt following recommended procedures:

Always access your Bitcoin exchange account or carry out transactions using a secure internet connection to reduce the likelihood of having your data intercepted or your account hacked.

Whenever it is possible, turn on the Two-Factor Authentication (2FA) feature on both your exchange account and your wallet. In addition to your password, a second form of verification, such as an unique code that is produced on your smartphone, is required in order to access accounts protected by two-factor authentication (2FA).

Maintain regular backups of your wallet, and save the backup phrase or seed in a secure location outside of your wallet. This assures that you will still be able to restore your wallet in the event that it is lost, stolen, or if the hardware it uses malfunctions. Make sure to evaluate the functionality of the recovery procedure once you have completed the steps outlined in the backup instructions provided by your wallet provider.

Implement additional security precautions such as making use of strong and unique passwords, ensuring that your wallet software is always up to date, enabling encryption if it is available, and being wary of phishing attempts and strange connections.

When you are ready to make your first Bitcoin purchase, you should make sure that you have selected a trustworthy exchange, created a safe wallet, and done any other necessary security procedures. Proceed in the following manner:

You can fund your exchange account with any of the available payment options, such as a bank transfer, credit or debit card, or transfer of another cryptocurrency. When depositing funds, make sure to follow the guidelines that are supplied by the exchange.

You will need to go to the trading part of the platform where you are exchanging currency and then select the option to buy Bitcoin. Before committing to the purchase, make sure to enter the desired quantity and examine the order's specifics. Make sure to take a note of any fees that are associated with completing the transaction.

Wait for the transaction to be completed and confirmed on the blockchain after your order has been successfully placed and confirmed. Congestion on the network and the rules of the chosen exchange both have an impact on the amount of time required for the confirmation process.

Once the transaction has been finalized, you should move the Bitcoin you purchased from the exchange into your own personal Bitcoin wallet so that it can be stored safely. To start the transfer process, it is necessary to follow the instructions that were provided by the provider of your wallet.

The world of Bitcoin and other cryptocurrencies is one that is always moving forward and experiencing change. Education and awareness should be a top priority if you want to stay informed and make judgments that are informed. Maintain an up-to-date knowledge of the latest information, advancements, and best practices by consulting reliable sources. Be aware of the dangers that come with investing in Bitcoin, never put in more money than you can afford to lose and give some thought to seeking tailored assistance from a professional financial advisor.

Purchasing your first Bitcoin can be an experience that is both thrilling and empowering. You will be able to confidently enter the world of cryptocurrencies once you have a knowledge of important ideas, selected a trustworthy exchange or platform, selected a safe Bitcoin wallet, ensured the protection of your funds, and followed the step-by-step instructions for completing your first purchase. Keep in mind that safety should be your top priority, that you should always be up to date on news, and that you should always invest responsibly. As you begin your adventure with Bitcoin, it is important that you recognize the transformational power of this technology and take pleasure in the advantages of being a participant in a decentralized financial ecosystem.

CHAPTER III
Navigating the Bitcoin Ecosystem

Exploring different types of Bitcoin wallets

Bitcoin wallets are essential tools for safely storing and managing your digital assets. They may be downloaded from the Bitcoin website. It is crucial to have a solid understanding of the different kinds of Bitcoin wallets that are accessible, especially with the continued rise in Bitcoin's level of popularity. In this section, we will discuss a variety of Bitcoin wallets, such as software wallets (desktop, mobile, and web-based), hardware wallets, paper wallets, and multisignature wallets. Software wallets can be used on desktop computers, mobile devices, and the web. In terms of choosing a Bitcoin wallet, we are going to look into their features, benefits, and security factors in order to guide you in making an educated choice.

Software wallets make it easy to access and manage your Bitcoin assets and are highly recommended. Desktop wallets, such as Bitcoin Core and Electrum, provide you complete control over your private keys and create a risk-free setting for conducting Bitcoin transactions. Because of their portability and simplicity of operation, mobile wallets such as Electrum and Mycelium are ideally suited for use in regular financial dealings. Wallets hosted on the internet, such as Coinbase and Blockchain.com, may be accessed via a web browser, giving you the ability to manage your Bitcoin holdings from a variety of devices. Web-based wallets, on the other hand, are dependent on the security measures taken by the provider of the service.

A tangible device known as a hardware wallet is designed to keep your private keys offline. They add an additional degree of protection by preventing potential internet dangers from coming into contact with your keys. Hardware wallets, like as Trezor, Ledger, and KeepKey, generate and store private keys within the device itself. These private keys are used to access the wallet. Transactions are digitally signed within the hardware wallet, guaranteeing that private keys are never exported from the device in any way. Bitcoin holders who intend to keep their funds for an extended period of time often use hardware wallets because they provide an optimal level of protection without sacrificing usability.

Paper wallets provide an offline storage solution for Bitcoin holdings that are held for an extended period of time. They need you to print your private keys and the associated Bitcoin addresses on a physical medium, most often paper. Paper wallets offer a high level of protection because their private keys are stored offline, away from any possible threats that the internet may pose. However, as a result of the physical form of the items, they are prone to being damaged, lost, or stolen. The generation of paper wallets ought to take place on dependable and protected platforms, as this will protect the authenticity of the created keys.

Bitcoin transactions can only be authorized by multisignature wallets if more than one signature is provided. They provide an increased level of security and protection against theft by requiring the participation of numerous parties before a transaction can be initiated. Wallets that support multiple signatures, or multisig, are especially helpful for joint bank accounts and businesses that need several people to sign off on each transaction. Multisig wallets provide an extra layer of security, protection against single points of failure, and enhanced transparency for shared accounts. This is accomplished by sharing signing authority among numerous parties.

When choosing a Bitcoin wallet, there are a few important considerations that should be made:

Give high priority to wallets that offer strong security features like as control over private keys, encryption, and the option to backup and recover your wallet. Evaluate the provider of the wallet in terms of their reputation and track record, as well as their dedication to the best security procedures.

Think on the requirements you have for ease of access and convenience. A mobile wallet is an option to consider if you do a lot of business while you're on the move. It's possible that a hardware wallet is the best option for someone who places an importance on safety. Conduct an assessment of your way of life and the things that are important to you in order to locate the optimal convenience and safety compromise.

Conduct an analysis of the user experience as well as the UI of the wallet. Make sure that the wallet is user-friendly, has a simple interface, and provides trustworthy customer care in the event that you experience any difficulties. Your whole Bitcoin experience can be improved by using a wallet that is simple to use.

It is essential for the safe management of your digital assets that you become familiar with the many types of Bitcoin wallets. Various wallet kinds, include hardware wallets and software wallets, paper wallets, and multisignature wallets, each provide a different amount of ease, security, and authority over your private keys. When selecting a Bitcoin wallet, it is important to take into account the following factors: security features, ease, accessibility, user experience, and support. Make safety a top priority by creating backups of your wallet on a regular basis and according to best practices. You will be able to confidently select a Bitcoin wallet that meets your criteria and handle your digital assets without experiencing any anxiety if you first have a grasp of the available possibilities and then align those options with your unique requirements.

Understanding Bitcoin addresses and private keys

In the realm of Bitcoin, it is absolutely necessary to have a solid understanding of the concepts of addresses and private keys in order to effectively manage and protect your digital assets. Bitcoin addresses are used as the public identity, which enables you to receive funds. Private keys, on the other hand, are the secret keys that provide proof of ownership and make it possible to conduct transactions securely. In this section, we will look into the complexities of Bitcoin addresses and private keys, including their responsibilities, cryptographic concepts, address forms, and the relevance of secure administration. Specifically, we will focus on how Bitcoin addresses are formatted. You will be able to confidently traverse the world of Bitcoin and safeguard your digital wealth if you have a thorough understanding of these key ideas.

Bitcoin addresses are alphanumeric identifiers that are made up of letters and numbers, and they serve as a user's public identification within the Bitcoin network. They are the final point of contact for Bitcoin transactions and are an essential component in the process of receiving payments. Bitcoin addresses are generated by using a combination of difficult mathematical operations and cryptographic methods. This ensures that each address is completely unique and that it is kept secure. These addresses can be found in a variety of formats, such as legacy addresses beginning with a "1," SegWit addresses beginning with a "3," and Bech32 addresses beginning with a "bc1." Users are able to select the choice that is most suited to their requirements because each format possesses its own set of benefits as well as compatibility issues.

Your Bitcoin holdings are only accessible through the use of a private key, which is a string of lengthy numbers that are produced at random. They are derived from cryptographic algorithms, the most common of which is known as Elliptic Curve Cryptography (ECC). Signing transactions and establishing ownership requires the use of private keys, which are required for this purpose. Bitcoin addresses are generated using public keys; however, private keys are not made public and must be maintained in a secure location. The fact that losing possession of your private keys can result in the loss of your Bitcoin holdings highlights how important it is to prevent these keys from being accessed in an unauthorized manner.

Bitcoin addresses and private keys are closely related in terms of their cryptographic properties. Bitcoin addresses are formed from public keys, which are derived from the corresponding private keys in the Bitcoin network. The relationship between addresses and private keys is one-way, which means that you cannot derive the private key from the address or the public key. This is an essential point to keep in mind, since it is crucial to highlight. The security and integrity of Bitcoin transactions are protected by this relationship, which only goes in one direction. When spending Bitcoin from a specific address or transferring Bitcoin from one address to another, you are required to provide ownership proof by giving a valid signature generated with the associated private key. This cryptographic verification assures that only the legitimate owner of a particular Bitcoin address may access and handle the funds linked with that address.

It is absolutely necessary to ensure the safety of your Bitcoin addresses and private keys if you wish to guard your digital funds. The following behaviors add to their sense of safety:

It is absolutely necessary to create backups of your private keys and related addresses on a regular basis in order to protect them from being lost or destroyed. Paper wallets, hardware wallets, or digital backups that are securely encrypted can all be used as methods of data preservation. You can guarantee that you can still access and retrieve your funds even if one copy of your private key is destroyed or lost by producing redundant copies of it and storing them in other locations.

Your private keys and addresses will not be accessible through the internet when you store them using an offline storage technique, which adds another layer of protection to your data. Popular options for cold storage include hardware wallets, which are essentially physical devices created specifically for the purpose of safely keeping private keys, as well as paper wallets, in which the private key is printed out on paper. You can secure your private keys from potential online dangers like hacking and viruses if you store them in a location that is not connected to the internet.

It is absolutely necessary to make use of secure equipment and connections whenever you access your addresses or private keys. It is best to avoid using public computers or networks that you are not familiar with, as doing so could put the security of your keys at risk. Make sure that none of your devices are infected with malicious software and that all of your connections are encrypted and secure. You can reduce the likelihood that unauthorized parties will have access to your private keys if you take precautions and follow established access policies.

A further degree of protection can be added to your Bitcoin wallet by changing your Bitcoin addresses on a regular basis and producing new key pairs. This method lessens the danger that comes with key exposure over a prolonged period of time and improves privacy in general. You can make it more difficult for possible attackers to monitor your transaction history and correlate it with a single address or key by constantly creating fresh addresses and key pairings. This makes it more difficult for potential attackers to steal your cryptocurrency.

It is absolutely necessary to have a solid understanding of Bitcoin addresses and private keys in order to efficiently manage and protect your digital wealth. Bitcoin addresses are used as the public identity, which enables you to receive funds. Private keys, on the other hand, are the secret keys that provide proof of ownership and make it possible to conduct transactions securely. You can reduce the likelihood of having your Bitcoin holdings stolen and assure their long-term safety if you adopt key rotation and secure management of your Bitcoin addresses and private keys. This can be accomplished through the use of backup and recovery procedures, cold storage solutions, secure access protocols, and other similar activities. Keep in mind that the secure storage of your private keys is very necessary for you to continue exercising control over, and ownership of, your digital wealth in the decentralized world of Bitcoin.

Using Bitcoin for transactions

Bitcoin, which functions as a decentralized digital currency, has fundamentally altered the manner in which transactions are carried out. Bitcoin has gained appeal among individuals and businesses all over the world due to the distinctive qualities it possesses, which include transparency, security, and the fact that it is borderless. In this section, we will explore the process of utilizing Bitcoin for transactions, including its advantages and disadvantages, the steps required in sending and receiving Bitcoin, the function of wallets and addresses, the fees associated with Bitcoin transactions, and the ever-changing landscape of Bitcoin payments. Individuals and companies are able to take advantage of the possibilities presented by this innovative form of digital currency if they have a thorough understanding of how Bitcoin can be used for financial transactions.

Transactions based on Bitcoin entail the transfer of value from one party to another through the use of the Bitcoin network. They do this by utilizing cryptographic techniques in conjunction with the decentralized nature of the blockchain to ensure that all transactions are secure, immutable, and transparent. Bitcoin transactions offer a number of advantages over traditional payment methods, including faster settlement times, decreased fees, global accessibility, and enhanced privacy in comparison to existing banking institutions.

Bitcoin wallets are essentially digital safe deposit boxes that can be used for the management and storage of Bitcoins. They are available in a variety of formats, such as desktop, mobile, and web-based software wallets, as well as hardware wallets, paper wallets, and multisignature wallets. Wallets give users the ability to build and manage Bitcoin addresses, which serve as unique identifiers for receiving funds and can be generated by the user. Bitcoin addresses are essential for identifying the recipient of a transaction since they are obtained from public keys. These keys are distributed publicly.

To be able to send Bitcoin, the wallet of the sender needs to have a sufficient balance in it. They need the Bitcoin address of the recipient, which may be obtained by either the sender and receiver exchanging their respective unique Bitcoin addresses or by scanning a QR code. The transaction is generated and signed by the sender's wallet with the sender's private key, providing a cryptographic proof that ownership was maintained. After then, the transaction that has been signed is broadcasted to the Bitcoin network, where miners validate and verify it before it is included to a block.

The sender must have the receiver's Bitcoin address in order for the recipient to receive Bitcoin. This address may be shown in the form of a string of text or it may be encoded in a QR code for the purpose of making it easier to scan. When the sender begins the transaction, it immediately becomes part of a pool of others that have not yet been confirmed. Miners validate individual transactions before choosing which ones to include in a block. Once a miner successfully mines a block that contains the transaction, the transaction is regarded as confirmed, it is made visible in the wallet of the recipient, and it is put to the blockchain to ensure that it cannot be altered.

Transaction fees are a common cost associated with Bitcoin transactions. These costs provide an incentive for miners to prioritize the inclusion of these transactions in blocks. The amount of the cost is decided by a number of parameters, including the transaction size, the level of network congestion, and the required confirmation speed. The amount of time required for confirmation can change depending on the state of the network. The finality of Bitcoin transactions is normally determined by the completion of a number of confirmations, the length of which is determined by the fees associated with the transaction, the amount of network congestion, and the desired level of security.

Benefits such as lower transaction costs and increased customer reach are driving a steady increase in the number of merchants that are adopting Bitcoin. Bitcoin's use has increased as a result of the growing number of major businesses, online retailers, and service providers that now accept it as a form of payment. Payment processors enable Bitcoin transactions between merchants and customers, changing Bitcoin payments into traditional currencies if the merchant so chooses, and offering businesses with options that are more streamlined. The layer-2 scaling solution known as the Lightning Network was created on top of the Bitcoin blockchain. It enables quick transactions at a cheap cost through payment channels, which improves Bitcoin's ability to scale and encourages its use in everyday transactions.

The use of Bitcoin for financial transactions has a wide range of advantages, some of which are accelerated transaction settlement times, decreased fees, global accessibility, and greater anonymity. Individuals and companies gain the ability to capitalize on the promise of this innovative digital currency by gaining an understanding of the steps required to send and receive Bitcoins, the function of wallets and addresses, the fees associated with Bitcoin transactions, and the changing landscape of Bitcoin payments. The influence that Bitcoin is having on the world's financial system is having the effect of changing traditional payment methods by offering a decentralized and efficient alternative for conducting transactions. Individuals and companies alike can open themselves up to a world of opportunities and benefit from the revolutionary potential of digital currency if they adopt Bitcoin.

Sending and receiving Bitcoin payments

With its decentralized and effective means of completing transactions, Bitcoin has emerged as a disruptive force in the world of finance. It's vital to comprehend the nuances of sending and receiving Bitcoin payments if you want to succeed in this digital environment. This section will examine the steps involved in a Bitcoin transaction, including the function of wallets and addresses, transaction confirmation, and security issues. We will also talk about how Bitcoin payments are developing, including merchant acceptance and the incorporation of the Lightning Network. Understanding the complexities of Bitcoin payments will enable both consumers and organizations to take full benefit of this innovative digital currency's capabilities.

Value is transferred from one party to another across the Bitcoin network during a transaction. These transactions are documented on the blockchain, a public ledger that is open and unchangeable. When compared to conventional payment methods, Bitcoin transactions have a number of benefits, including quicker settlement times, lower fees, accessibility on a worldwide scale, and improved privacy.

Bitcoin is managed and stored digitally through Bitcoin wallets. They can be found in a variety of formats, including hardware wallets, paper wallets, multisignature wallets, and software wallets (desktop, mobile, and web-based). Users can create and manage Bitcoin addresses in wallets, which serve as distinctive identifiers for receiving funds.

A significant wallet balance as well as the recipient's Bitcoin address are required for sending Bitcoin. The recipient's address, the amount of Bitcoin to send, and any other information are entered into the sender's wallet to generate a transaction. The sender's private key is then used to digitally sign the transaction, establishing ownership in a secure manner. The Bitcoin network broadcasts this signed transaction, and miners check its validity.

The recipient provides the sender with their Bitcoin address in order to receive Bitcoin. The address can be shown as a series of characters or conveniently scanned as a QR code. The transaction enters a pool of unconfirmed transactions whenever the sender starts it. In order to guarantee their immutability, miners choose transactions from this pool, verify them, and add them to a block on the blockchain.

In order to prevent fraud and unauthorized access, security is essential in Bitcoin transactions. Bitcoin transactions are authorized by private keys, which must be safeguarded and kept in a secure location. Strong security protections are offered by options including hardware wallets, paper wallets, and encrypted digital backups. Additionally, ensuring the integrity of Bitcoin transactions depends on network security and avoiding fraud and scams.

Bitcoin use by businesses is still increasing, due to advantages like lower transaction costs and a larger consumer base. Bitcoin's utility has increased as a result of integration as a payment option by large businesses, internet merchants, and service providers. Payment processors make Bitcoin transactions easier for businesses and customers by assuring smooth transactions and, if needed, converting Bitcoin payments into more conventional currencies. A layer-2 scaling solution called the Lightning Network improves the scalability of Bitcoin by enabling quick and inexpensive transactions through payment systems.

Bitcoin payments provide both individuals and companies a revolutionary way to conduct financial transactions. The way we conduct business is changing as a result of Bitcoin's efficiency, speed, and worldwide accessibility. Individuals and organizations may fully utilize the potential of this innovative digital currency by knowing the steps involved in Bitcoin transactions, the function of wallets and addresses, transaction confirmation, security considerations, and the changing environment of Bitcoin payments. Bitcoin's influence on the world's financial system is expected to transform established payment systems by providing a decentralized and effective alternative for transactions as use of the cryptocurrency rises.

CHAPTER
IV
Bitcoin Mining and the Blockchain

How Bitcoin mining works

For transaction validation, network security, and the creation of new Bitcoins, bitcoin mining, a crucial procedure in the world of cryptocurrencies, is necessary. This section seeks to explore the intricate processes of Bitcoin mining, including its motivations, miners' roles, the block validation procedure, the consensus mechanism, mining hardware and software, and its effects on the environment. A greater understanding of the technology underlying this revolutionary digital currency can be gained by understanding the inner workings of Bitcoin mining.

Network security and new Bitcoin issuance are the two main goals of Bitcoin mining. By taking part in the mining process, users contribute to the security and reliability of the Bitcoin network, reducing fraud and preserving user confidence. Newly created Bitcoins are also given to miners as payment, incentivizing their participation.

Within the Bitcoin network, miners carry out crucial responsibilities. They verify transactions to make sure they are genuine and follow the network's rules. In addition, Proof-of-Work (PoW) algorithms are challenging mathematical problems that miners compete to solve in order to generate new blocks that include batches of validated transactions. Miners help the network's participants maintain consensus in this way.

To validate the validity of transactions and add new blocks to the blockchain, miners must complete a number of stages known as block validation. In order to solve the PoW puzzle, they choose unconfirmed transactions from the mempool, build the block header, modify the nonce value, and broadcast the verified block to the network. The validity of the block is later checked by additional miners before they include it in their local copy of the blockchain.

Bitcoin miners use specialized hardware and software to carry out their mining operations. Application-Specific Integrated Circuits (ASICs), a type of mining hardware, are made specifically to carry out the complex computations necessary to solve PoW algorithms. Mining software automates transaction validation and block formation, promotes connection with other nodes, and controls the mining process.

Concerns regarding the environmental impact of Bitcoin mining have been raised because to its energy usage. Mining operations demand a huge amount of computational power, which results in a significant amount of electricity consumption, especially in areas where the generation of energy is dominated by fossil fuels. However, steps are being taken to address this problem. By switching to renewable energy sources, some miners are lowering their carbon footprint. Additionally, research is concentrated on creating mining equipment that uses less energy and enhancing mining algorithms.

Bitcoin mining is essential for the creation of new Bitcoins, network security, and transaction validation. People can obtain a thorough grasp of this novel process by comprehending the function of mining, the role of miners, the block validation procedure, the hardware and software involved, and the environmental impact. Although mining has problems with regard to energy consumption, continuous initiatives to improve energy efficiency and adopt renewable energy sources aim to reduce its environmental impact. The inventive potential of digital currencies and their capacity to change the nature of the global financial system are demonstrated by Bitcoin mining.

Mining hardware and software options

A key component of the digital currency ecosystem, cryptocurrency mining relies on specialized technology and software. As mining technology has advanced, it now provides a variety of solutions to satisfy miners' growing needs. The complexity of mining hardware and software alternatives, as well as their features, benefits, and drawbacks, will be examined in this section. People can maximize their mining potential and make educated selections if they are aware of the nuances of mining equipment.

The term "mining hardware" describes specialized machinery made to carry out the complex computations necessary for cryptocurrency mining. It significantly contributes to the efficiency and computing power of mining operations, which is essential to their success. Central Processing Units (CPUs), Graphics Processing Units (GPUs), and Application-Specific Integrated Circuits (ASICs) are the three main categories of mining hardware.

Although once the preferred option for mining, CPUs have lost some of their efficiency due to their multipurpose nature. The parallel processing capability of GPUs, which were first created for gaming and multimedia applications, make them suited for mining. ASICs, on the other hand, are custom-designed devices made just for mining cryptocurrencies and offer unmatched hashing power and energy efficiency.

Each form of mining equipment has benefits and drawbacks. Despite their versatility, CPUs are no longer competitive for mining Bitcoin. They are still usable for mining some altcoins, though. Due to their flexibility and parallel processing capacity, GPUs are popular among miners and are excellent for mining a variety of cryptocurrencies.

Due to their superior performance and specialized design, ASICs predominate in Bitcoin mining.

The Bitcoin network and mining devices are connected by mining software. It enables miners to manage tasks and keep track of performance while connecting to mining pools. There are numerous possibilities:

A full copy of the blockchain may be downloaded and maintained by miners using full node software like Bitcoin Core, which increases network security and decentralization.

By collaborating and pooling their computational power, miners can use mining pool software to increase their chances of winning rewards. Coordination and distribution of tasks among participating miners is facilitated by mining pool software like CGMiner and BFGMiner.

For the purpose of mining cryptocurrencies, specialized mining operating systems like EthOS, SimpleMining, and HiveOS have been created. These systems include easy-to-use user interfaces, mining management tools, and increased mining rig stability.

Options for mining gear and software are always changing as a result of new developments in technology. ASIC manufacturers frequently introduce new models with enhanced performance and efficiency. The power and efficiency of GPUs are also improving. New features are incorporated into mining software to increase productivity and profitability.

When choosing mining equipment, miners must take into account a number of things. The initial expenditure, electricity use, and possible profitability are all costs to take into account. Because different cryptocurrencies use different mining algorithms and because different types of hardware and software may not be compatible with each other, mining algorithm compatibility is crucial.

For best mining results, selecting the appropriate hardware and software is essential. Cost, compatibility, computational power, and energy efficiency must all be taken into account. To stay competitive in the fast-paced world of cryptocurrency mining, miners must keep up with technological breakthroughs.

The full potential of cryptocurrency mining can be unlocked by choosing the right hardware and software combination, whether using GPUs for altcoin mining, ASICs for Bitcoin mining, or specialized mining software for effective administration. By utilizing the appropriate mining equipment, miners can effectively engage in this dynamic ecosystem and contribute to the expansion and security of the world of digital currencies.

Joining a mining pool

Mining cryptocurrency today requires a lot of resources and is competitive. Joining a mining pool has emerged as an option since individual miners struggle to earn consistent returns. By pooling their computational resources, miners can increase their odds of successfully mining blocks and obtaining rewards. This section examines the idea of mining pools, their benefits, how to join a pool, prominent mining pool options, and factors to take into account while choosing the best pool. Individuals can increase their mining profitability and actively engage in the Bitcoin mining community by knowing the mechanics of mining pools.

Collaborative platforms called mining pools allow individual miners to combine their computational power and mine blocks together. This strategy has a number of benefits. As miners contribute to the group mining effort, it first enhances the possibility of obtaining rewards. Second, compared to solo mining, which might be impacted by mining difficulty and luck, mining pools offer more reliable returns. Through mining pools, miners may also access real-time statistics, keep an eye on their progress, and get technical support.

Miners must do extensive research, choose a trustworthy pool, establish an account, set up their mining software, and connect to the mining server of the pool in order to join a mining pool.

When evaluating different mining pools, miners should consider factors such pool size, mining costs, reward options, reputation, and community support. Online forums and pool comparison websites can offer helpful advice for choosing the best pool.

By giving the required details, including an email address, username, and password, miners create an account with the selected pool. For security reasons, some pools could demand additional verification procedures.

To connect to the mining pool, miners set up their mining software. The IP, port number, and credentials for the pool's mining server must be specified. Each mining program has a unique setting procedure that, depending on the requirements of the particular pool, may also include other parameters.

By starting their mining program with the specified settings, miners begin the connection to the pool. Miners can contribute their processing capacity to the group mining effort by connecting through the program to the pool's mining server.

Slush Pool, F2Pool, and Antpool are just a few of the well-known mining pools that are available. Slush pool is one of the first mining pools that provides dependability and transparency. It makes use of a score-based reward system that takes into consideration a miner's cumulative efforts. Bitcoin as well as other cryptocurrencies can be mined with Slush Pool.

One of the biggest mining pools in the world is F2Pool, commonly known as Discus Fish. It supports a number of cryptocurrencies and uses a pay-per-share (PPS) reward mechanism to ensure miners receive regular payouts. The trustworthy service and strong infrastructure of F2Pool are well known.

One of the largest Bitcoin mining pools is Antpool, run by Bitmain. It offers variable reward options and supports different mining algorithms. With the help of Antpool's PPS+ and Full Pay-Per-Share (FPPS) reward systems, miners can expect a steady income.

When choosing a mining pool, miners should take a number of things into account.

The size and distribution of a pool's hashrate can affect mining productivity and payouts. While smaller pools may provide bigger rewards with higher fluctuation, larger pools often give more constant payments. Based on their level of risk tolerance and preferred mining experience, miners should strike a balance.

Typically, mining pools deduct a fee from the rewards given to miners in exchange for their services. Miners should compare fee schedules and take into account how they relate to the characteristics, dependability, and payout consistency of the pool.

Different compensation strategies are used by mining pools, including Pay-Per-Share (PPS), Pay-Per-Last-N-Shares (PPLNS), and Score-Based systems. Understanding the payout strategies used by a pool will help miners decide which one best suits their tastes and mining objectives.

A more dependable mining experience is guaranteed when you join a respected and established pool. Miners should take into account a pool's reputation, involvement with the community, and assistance offered to its members.

Individual miners have the chance to increase their mining profitability through collaborative mining by joining a mining pool. Miners improve their chances of successfully mining blocks and obtaining rewards by sharing processing power. Thorough research, choosing a reliable pool, setting up an account, configuring mining software, and connecting to the pool's mining server are all steps in the procedure.

When choosing a mining pool, miners should take into account elements including pool size, hashrate distribution, mining fees, payout methods, reputation, and community support. Miners can select a pool that fits their mining objectives, risk tolerance, and desired level of reward consistency by carefully weighing these aspects. Joining a mining pool provides a sense of camaraderie and support within the Bitcoin mining environment in addition to increasing the likelihood of receiving rewards. Individuals can actively participate in the cryptocurrency mining community while increasing their mining profitability by using mining pools for collaborative mining.

The role of the blockchain in securing Bitcoin transactions

The blockchain is the foundational technology for the decentralized digital currency Bitcoin, which depends on it to secure transactions. A visible and unchangeable public ledger that records all Bitcoin transactions is provided by the blockchain. The fundamental function of the blockchain in protecting Bitcoin transactions is examined in this section. It digs into the blockchain's essential elements, such as the consensus and transaction verification methods, as well as how the blockchain affects trust and security within the Bitcoin ecosystem and how it resists fraud and manipulation. People may grasp the importance of the blockchain in establishing a secure and reliable system for Bitcoin transactions by knowing its function.

All Bitcoin transactions are tracked by the distributed ledger known as the blockchain. It operates as a chain of blocks that is transparent and immutable, with each block containing a set of transactions. A decentralized network of computers which are also known as nodes is responsible for updating and maintaining the blockchain. The system's security and dependability are aided by its transparency and immutability.

A key component of protecting Bitcoin transactions is transaction verification. A transaction must first go through validation before it can be posted to the blockchain. The transaction's authenticity is confirmed by miners or validating nodes, who make sure it follows the guidelines of the Bitcoin protocol and that the sender has sufficient funds. To reach consensus among nodes regarding the sequence and validity of transactions, consensus techniques such as Proof-of-Work (PoW) or Proof-of-Stake (PoS) are essential. These controls safeguard the blockchain's integrity and stop double spending.

The integrity of Bitcoin transactions is guaranteed by the blockchain, which is built to withstand fraud and tampering. Each block in an irreversible chain is connected to the previous block using cryptographic hash algorithms. Because of this connection, it is very challenging for attackers to change earlier transactions covertly. The distributed structure of the blockchain, where several copies are maintained across a network of nodes, adds an additional layer of protection. It is almost hard to change a transaction in one copy of the blockchain without also affecting it in all versions. The blockchain is shielded against malicious assaults and manipulation by its consensus-based security paradigm.

Within the Bitcoin ecosystem, the blockchain is crucial in building trust and security. The blockchain allows for direct peer-to-peer transactions, doing away with middlemen like banks or payment processors, minimizing dependency on third parties. Anyone may verify and audit transactions due to the blockchain's transparency and auditability. By allowing users to independently verify the integrity of the system, this transparency promotes trust within the ecosystem. The consensus mechanism and built-in security features of the technology establish a trustless system due to the blockchain. Participants can conduct transactions without having to put their mutual trust in one another by relying on the blockchain's security and transparency.

Ongoing improvements and security controls are being put in place to further boost the blockchain's security and effectiveness. Segregated Witness (SegWit), a protocol update that separates transaction signatures from the transaction data, is an example of such a measure. This update increases transaction capacity and reduces some threats. Additionally, layer-2 solutions like the

Lightning Network seek to improve the Bitcoin network's scalability and anonymity. These innovations make it possible to conduct off-chain transactions more quickly and cheaply while still utilizing the inherent security of the underlying blockchain.

The blockchain supports the whole Bitcoin network and offers a safe and open ledger for transaction recording. The blockchain maintains the legality and integrity of transactions through its verification and consensus methods, reducing the danger of fraud and manipulation. It is extremely resistant to attacks and manipulation because of its distributed architecture and cryptographic characteristics. The blockchain's transparency and lack of intermediaries promote trust and allow for safe transactions. The security and scalability of the blockchain are further improved by current advancements and security mechanisms like SegWit and layer-2 solutions.

People are better equipped to accept the possibilities of this innovative technology when they comprehend the crucial function that the blockchain plays in protecting Bitcoin transactions. The blockchain paves the way for a future where digital transactions are more secure, decentralized, and built on trust. The blockchain will remain at the forefront as the Bitcoin ecosystem develops, assuring the security, transparency, and reliability of transactions in the online world.

CHAPTER
V
Bitcoin Security and Privacy

Best practices for securing your Bitcoin

Securing digital assets has become of utmost importance as Bitcoin obtains wider acceptance and value. Although Bitcoin is built on strong cryptographic security and decentralized principles, users still need to take extra precautions to safeguard their holdings. The best techniques for protecting Bitcoin are examined in this section, including secure wallets, reliable authentication procedures, backup plans, and being vigilant for fraud and social engineering. People may increase the security of their Bitcoin holdings and confidently navigate the cryptocurrency ecosystem by putting these ideas into practice.

It is essential to be aware of the various risks and threats related to digital assets in order to secure Bitcoin efficiently. Bitcoin is a desirable target for hackers and cybercriminals due to factors including its value and digital nature. Having a proactive security strategy requires being aware of typical dangers including phishing scams, malware, hacked wallets, and social engineering.

Securing Bitcoin starts with picking the best wallet. There are different levels of security and practicality offered by various wallet types, including hardware wallets, software wallets, and paper wallets. An additional layer of protection is added by implementing multi-signature wallets that demand multiple private keys for transaction authorization. Furthermore, keeping private keys away from any online threats by adopting cold storage techniques like hardware wallets or paper wallets or offline storage of Bitcoin further improves security.

Protecting Bitcoin holdings requires the use of strong authentication procedures. For wallet accounts and related services, secure and distinctive passwords must be created. A further degree of security is offered by two-factor authentication (2FA), which calls for a second form of identification, such as a verification code delivered to a mobile device. When accessing wallets or conducting transactions, biometric identification techniques like fingerprint or facial recognition offer convenience and increased security.

It's critical to regularly backup Bitcoin wallets and private keys to guard against data loss, hardware malfunctions, and theft. The possibility to recover Bitcoin holdings in an emergency is ensured by creating encrypted backups and storing them safely in several places. When using cloud storage for backups, caution should be taken to apply strong encryption and select reliable providers with strict safety measures. The integrity of backups is regularly verified, and the capacity to restore Bitcoin holdings when necessary is confirmed.

Holders of Bitcoin must be on the lookout for fraud and social engineering strategies. People are better able to identify and steer clear of fraudulent schemes when they are knowledgeable on the most recent scams and phishing strategies. It is essential to check the legitimacy of websites, links, and software downloads before disclosing important information or conducting business. Individuals should guard against potential compromise by using caution when handling private information and avoiding distributing private keys, wallet recovery phrases, or sensitive information through unsecure means.

It's crucial to keep wallet software and related programs up to date with the most recent security patches. The risk of virus or hacking attempts is decreased by using secure and up-to-date operating systems on devices used for Bitcoin transactions. The early identification of suspicious behavior and potential security breaches is made possible by routinely monitoring wallet transactions and account activities.

When communicating with Bitcoin-related services, using encrypted communication channels like Virtual Private Networks (VPNs) or secure messaging apps adds an added layer of security. To avoid any eavesdropping or malicious activity, caution should be used when utilizing public Wi-Fi networks to access Bitcoin wallets or conduct transactions.

Planning a digital inheritance makes ensuring that members or beneficiaries are aware of any Bitcoin assets and their login information. Making secure records of security practices and recovery data aids family members in navigating the challenges of inheriting Bitcoin holdings.

Bitcoin security demands a thorough and proactive strategy. For security measures to be put in place effectively, it is essential to understand the risks and dangers related to digital assets. People can safeguard their Bitcoin holdings by using secure wallet procedures, putting in place strong authentication mechanisms, developing routine backup plans, and being vigilant for scams and social engineering. The total security posture is further improved by consistent security updates, secure communication methods, and beneficiary and family education.

It is essential to keep up with new risks as the Bitcoin ecosystem develops and to adjust security procedures accordingly. Individuals can navigate the Bitcoin landscape with confidence by following these best practices since they will know their digital assets are well-protected in the face of potential threats and difficulties. Maintaining a commitment to security is necessary to protect Bitcoin, assuring the long-term preservation of digital wealth in the era of cryptocurrencies.

Protecting against hacks and scams

The growing popularity of cryptocurrency has opened the door to new opportunities, but it has also made people more vulnerable to a variety of threats, including the possibility of being hacked or scammed. Cybercriminals are utilizing increasingly sophisticated methods to take advantage of weaknesses and scam those who are unaware of the dangers they face as a result of the growth in the value of cryptocurrencies. In this section, we will discuss the most effective strategies for securing one's cryptocurrency holdings against attacks by hackers and con artists operating in the current environment. We will go over how to secure wallets and exchanges, how to spot typical frauds, how to build robust security measures, and how to stay informed about the changing threat landscape. Individuals are able to protect their digital assets and safely traverse the world of cryptocurrencies if they embrace these techniques and put them into practice.

The environment surrounding cryptocurrencies is loaded with dangers, and individuals need to be aware of the ever-shifting nature of the threats they face. Hackers are increasingly targeting individuals, exchanges, and wallets in an effort to obtain illegal access and steal digital assets, which has led to an increase in the number of cybersecurity concerns. It is absolutely necessary to gain an understanding of the nature of these dangers in order to successfully deploy security measures.

When it comes to guarding against hackers and frauds, securing digital wallets and exchanges is of the utmost importance. It is absolutely necessary to select wallet providers with a solid reputation that also implement strict safety precautions. By storing private keys offline and shielding them from internet dangers, the use of hardware wallets adds a further degree of protection to the user's cryptocurrency holdings. In order for individuals to keep their holdings safe when using cryptocurrency exchanges, they should look for platforms that have strong security mechanisms like as two-factor authentication (2FA) and cold storage.

Individuals need to be able to identify prevalent fraudulent schemes in order to protect themselves from being taken advantage of. Phishing attacks, in which con artists pretend to be a reputable websites or online services in an effort to deceive consumers into divulging critical information, are quite common. Individuals who are educated about the tactics of phishing are better able to protect themselves from falling for such cons. The cryptocurrency industry is filled with Ponzi scams and fraudulent initial coin offerings (ICOs), both of which are common. Individuals have a better chance of avoiding being taken advantage of by fraudulent schemes if they perform extensive research, verify the legality of projects, and exercise prudence when investing.

Individuals should employ strict security measures in order to strengthen the protection of their digital assets, as follows:

Before gaining access to accounts or carrying out transactions, enabling Two-Factor Authentication (2FA) adds an extra layer of protection by necessitating the use of a second verification method, which may take the form of an unique code that is sent to a mobile device.

It is easier to prevent unauthorized access if users choose strong, unique passwords and update such passwords on a regular basis. Utilizing a password manager can help you create and securely store passwords that are complicated and lengthy.

It is essential to regularly apply the most recent security patches to all software, including operating systems, applications, and anti-virus programs, as this is the best way to guard against known vulnerabilities.

When accessing services that are associated with cryptocurrencies, the use of Virtual Private Networks, or VPNs, enables a connection that is both encrypted and secure. This protects users from the possibility of eavesdropping and man-in-the-middle attacks.

It is absolutely necessary for those who want to secure their digital assets to be up to date on the most recent developments in cybersecurity trends and threats. Individuals get the ability to make decisions that are in their best interests and to keep one step ahead of potential dangers when they follow credible sources that supply accurate information. Individuals have the opportunity to get insight into developing scams and hacking techniques by engaging in community forums and participating in discussions. Individuals can get knowledge from other people's experiences by engaging in community forums. To keep one's security hygiene in good shape, it is essential to maintain a state of continuous learning and adapting to an ever-changing threat landscape.

In the world of cryptocurrencies, it is absolutely necessary to take precautions against hacks and scams. Individuals are able to effectively protect their digital assets if they have a thorough grasp of the risk landscape, secure wallets and exchanges, are aware of frequent frauds, put in place strict security measures, and keep themselves informed. It is important to maintain vigilance and proactivity at all times, modifying security methods in accordance with the shifting nature of the threat landscape. Individuals may successfully navigate the world of cryptocurrencies by adopting best practices and making a commitment to continual education. This will ensure the long-term security and integrity of their digital assets.

Privacy considerations when using Bitcoin

The growing popularity of Bitcoin as a decentralized and pseudonymous digital currency has given rise to conversations regarding the protection of individuals' privacy in the digital sphere. It is essential to have a solid understanding of the various privacy concerns that come into play while utilizing a cryptocurrency like Bitcoin, despite the fact that Bitcoin has certain privacy advantages over traditional financial systems. This section investigates the implications that utilizing Bitcoin has for users' privacy, as well as the transparency of the blockchain, potential threats to users' privacy, and effective methods for enhancing privacy. Individuals are able to strike a balance between the benefits of Bitcoin and the protection of their personal privacy if they have a thorough understanding of these factors and put appropriate protections into place.

Bitcoin transactions are pseudonymous, which means that they are not directly linked to the identities of the people conducting the transactions. Instead, each transaction is linked to an unique cryptographic address. Through the separation of transactional data and personal information that this feature provides, a level of privacy is provided.

The blockchain operates as a public ledger that keeps track of all transactions involving Bitcoins. The transparency of the blockchain makes it possible for anybody to access transaction details, including addresses and transaction amounts. This is despite the fact that the identities of users are not directly linked to one another. The complete protection of one's privacy is made more difficult by the existence of such transparency.

Address deanonymization is a privacy concern that can occur when techniques such as address clustering and network analysis are utilized. These approaches have the ability to reveal the connection that exists between Bitcoin addresses and actual identities. There are further risks to privacy posed by network surveillance and tracking of IP addresses, both of which have the potential to compromise the anonymity of Bitcoin users. In addition, the usage of centralized cryptocurrency exchanges, which frequently necessitate the completion of KYC procedures, may expose personally identifiable information to the risk of being compromised or misused.

When it comes to using Bitcoin, there are a few different best practices that may be implemented. By utilizing a variety of addresses for a variety of transactions, one can help obfuscate the patterns of those transactions and decrease the possibility of address linkage. The history of transactions may get obscured when using coin mixing and tumbling services, which makes it more difficult to track the flow of funds. The implementation of CoinJoin protocols makes it possible for numerous users to combine their individual transactions into a single transaction, which improves users' overall level of anonymity. Wallets with a focus on privacy, which include features such as HD wallets, Tor integration, and Coin Control, offer greater privacy features and safeguard against address reuse.

More privacy protections are available for Bitcoin transactions due to recent advancements in technology. Confidential Transactions use encryption to hide transaction amounts from anyone who could be looking over their shoulder. Users are able to validate transactions using zero-knowledge proofs without disclosing any sensitive information to the network. Both CoinSwap and the Lightning Network are designed to improve privacy and scalability by lowering the requirement for on-chain transactions while simultaneously supporting off-chain transactions.

While individuals should prioritize protecting their privacy, they should also be aware of the legal and regulatory obligations that come with using cryptocurrencies. It is becoming increasingly important to comply with legislation while also protecting one's privacy. It is equally important to strike a balance between protecting one's privacy and protecting one's financial security, given that increased privacy protections may reduce one's ability to recover lost funds or prevent fraudulent activities from occurring.

When it comes to protecting the privacy of one's personal information, the use of Bitcoin requires careful attention to privacy concerns. Users of Bitcoin should be aware of the potential hazards and implement best practices to safeguard their privacy, despite the fact that the pseudonymous nature of Bitcoin gives certain benefits to users' privacy. Personal information can be protected and the dangers associated with address linking and deanonymization can be reduced by adhering to privacy-enhancing habits, using numerous email addresses, using digital wallets and technologies that are designed with privacy in mind. It is essential to find an appropriate balance between protecting individuals' privacy and complying with applicable regulations, while also taking into account the potential effects on financial stability. Individuals can maximize their privacy while using the benefits of the Bitcoin network in the digital sphere if they understand these privacy considerations and take suitable precautions. This is possible because of the decentralized nature of the Bitcoin network.

Anonymity versus transparency in the Bitcoin network

Finding the ideal balance between anonymity and transparency inside the network has emerged as a unique difficulty as a result of the growth of Bitcoin and other cryptocurrencies. The openness of the blockchain raises concerns regarding the degree of privacy and the necessity of transparency in a decentralized financial system, even as Bitcoin grants pseudonymity and privacy to its users. The dynamics of anonymity and transparency in the Bitcoin network are examined in this section, along with their advantages and disadvantages, as well as the ongoing discussions about privacy, accountability, and regulatory compliance. People can gain understanding of the implications and take well-informed actions regarding their participation in the Bitcoin network by comprehending these principles.

The foundation of Bitcoin transactions is pseudonymity, or the idea that they are not directly connected to people in the real world. Transactions are instead linked to distinct cryptographic addresses, which offers a certain measure of privacy. But because the blockchain is a public ledger that keeps track of all Bitcoin transactions, anybody can see all transaction information, including addresses and transaction amounts. This openness guarantees accountability and prevents fraud.

In the Bitcoin network, anonymity has both advantages and disadvantages. On the one hand, financial privacy is safeguarded, keeping people's financial details private from prying eyes. The possibility of identity theft or targeted attacks is decreased by this confidentiality. Additionally, anonymity promotes freedom of expression, enabling people to conduct financial transactions without worrying about reprisal or censorship. In addition to protecting individual freedom and autonomy, anonymity can serve as a check on excessive surveillance.

On the other hand, anonymity can help with unlawful operations like money laundering and illicit business dealings. This presents difficulties for regulatory and law enforcement organizations trying to uphold financial integrity and stop illicit activity.

The blockchain's transparency comes with its own set of advantages and difficulties:

Within the Bitcoin network, transparency guarantees responsibility and confidence. Anyone can verify and audit each transaction that is recorded on the blockchain, creating a system of checks and balances. Due to the chronological record of transactions, this transparency also prevents double spending and upholds the security of the Bitcoin network. Additionally, because they can be tracked and identified, fraudulent behaviors are discouraged by publicly recorded transactions.

The transparency of the blockchain, however, prompts concerns about the disclosure of private financial data. The privacy of individuals may be violated by the public accessibility of transaction details, leaving them open to targeted attacks or unauthorized access.

Several privacy-enhancing technologies have evolved to solve the difficulties transparency poses:

Services for coin mixing and tumbling assist conceal transaction histories, making it challenging to track out where money came from. Confidential Transactions use cryptographic methods to encrypt transaction amounts, adding an extra layer of privacy while maintaining the integrity of the network. In order to balance privacy and openness, zero-knowledge proofs allow the validation of transactions without disclosing sensitive information.

The changing regulatory environment surrounding cryptocurrencies underscores the need to balance privacy concerns with the requirement for transparency and regulatory compliance. Governments and regulatory authorities work to prevent illegal activity while defending people's right to privacy. Anonymity and the prevention of financial crimes are reconciled by anti-money laundering (AML) rules. Understanding these perspectives enables people to navigate legal systems and adhere to legislation. Different nations have different views on privacy and transparency in the Bitcoin network.

Education is essential for navigating the difficulties of anonymity and transparency. Users of Bitcoin who are aware on the implications of anonymity and transparency are better equipped to make wise decisions and take proper steps to protect their privacy. In addition, users have a duty to use caution, abide by the law and morality, and strike a balance between privacy and transparency when interacting with the Bitcoin network.

The delicate balancing act between transparency and anonymity is demonstrated by the Bitcoin network. Financial privacy, freedom of speech, and surveillance restrictions are all made possible through anonymity. Accountability, trust, and the avoidance of fraudulent behaviors are all ensured by transparency. Technologies that guarantee privacy provide capabilities to improve confidentiality without affecting network integrity. Constant debate, updated laws, and user accountability are necessary to strike the ideal balance between privacy and accountability. Individuals can navigate the Bitcoin network while taking into account their privacy demands, regulatory compliance, and the larger societal implications of the decentralized financial environment by grasping the dynamics of anonymity and transparency.

CHAPTER
VI
Bitcoin Trading and Investing

Understanding Bitcoin price volatility

The first cryptocurrency, Bitcoin, has captured the attention of the financial community with its astounding price volatility. Investors and analysts have both been attracted and bewildered by the unpredictable nature of Bitcoin's price changes. This section will examine the idea of Bitcoin price volatility, looking at its causes, effects on adoption, and implications for investors and the cryptocurrency ecosystem as a whole. People can make informed judgments and navigate the unpredictable cryptocurrency market by understanding the dynamics of Bitcoin price volatility.

The term "Bitcoin price volatility" describes the swift and significant changes in the currency's value over very short periods of time. Statistical measurements like the standard deviation and volatility indexes are frequently used to quantify this volatility. Over the course of its existence, there have been substantial swings in the price of Bitcoin, with periods of quick growth and swift depreciation.

Bitcoin is vulnerable to market dynamics and speculative trading because of its large trading volume and relatively tiny market capitalization. Short-term price changes can be significantly influenced by market manipulation, investor sentiment, and news events.

The unstable price of Bitcoin is a result of its finite quantity and decentralized nature. The delicate equilibrium between supply and demand can be impacted by changes in demand, adoption rates, regulatory developments, and macroeconomic variables, which can result in price fluctuations.

Bitcoin lacks generally acknowledged fundamental valuation criteria, in contrast to conventional assets like equities or bonds. It is difficult to precisely estimate its inherent value in its absence, which increases price volatility. Uncertainty about Bitcoin's true worth leads to increased speculation and larger price swings.

For investors, the price volatility of Bitcoin offers both opportunities and threats. Because of the volatility's potential for big profits, it attracts speculators and investors who like taking risks. If not handled carefully, it also exposes investors to large losses. For navigating the volatility and reducing potential hazards, it's essential to implement risk management measures and adopt a long-term investment approach.

The adoption of Bitcoin as a means of exchange or a store of value may be hindered by its price volatility. Due to the potential impact on pricing and financial stability, businesses and individuals may be reluctant to embrace a currency with such high volatility. Stability and predictability are necessary for widespread adoption and mainstream acceptability, but they are difficult to achieve in the face of excessive price fluctuation.

Because of its price's inherent volatility, market manipulation and other fraudulent practices are made possible. Price movements can be used for personal advantage through manipulation techniques including pump-and-dump scams and fake news. Regulators are concerned about this, which highlights the need for strong regulatory frameworks to safeguard investors and preserve market integrity.

The nascent state of the cryptocurrency market is partially reflected in the volatility of the price of Bitcoin. Improved infrastructure, more transparent regulations, and higher liquidity may all result in less volatility as a market ages. More market stability may result from institutional investors' participation, the creation of Bitcoin derivatives, and the formation of trustworthy exchanges.

Using financial instruments like futures contracts and options, investors can lessen their exposure to the dangers brought on by the price fluctuations of Bitcoin. Market participants can hedge their positions and guard against unfavorable price changes using these instruments.

Stablecoins, or digital currencies backed by reliable assets like fiat money, seek to stabilize the cryptocurrency market and lessen volatility. Stablecoins offer a way to conduct transactions without being exposed to the price swings of cryptocurrencies like Bitcoin by delivering a consistent value.

The impact of Bitcoin price volatility on an investor's portfolio can be reduced by diversifying assets across several asset classes and implementing risk management techniques. People can reduce the potential negative effects of Bitcoin's volatility on their overall wealth by spreading risk and distributing assets among different investment vehicles.

Increased liquidity, regulatory certainty, and institutional adoption may all help to lessen price volatility as the Bitcoin market develops and matures. Institutional investors can be attracted and popular acceptance can be fostered by regulatory frameworks that safeguard investors and improve market stability.

The involvement of institutional investors and the creation of strong cryptocurrency exchanges can provide liquidity, which can help keep Bitcoin's price stable. More liquidity improves pricing efficiency and lessens the effect of individual deals on the market as a whole.

The development of trustworthy valuation models and fundamental measures that are unique to cryptocurrencies can help to provide a more thorough understanding of the intrinsic value of Bitcoin. Market participants can make more educated investment decisions and potentially lessen price volatility by creating explicit procedures for figuring out how much Bitcoin and other cryptocurrencies are worth.

The volatile price of Bitcoin continues to be its distinguishing feature. While it offers chances for substantial rewards, there are also risks as well as challenges for the regulatory and adoption frameworks. For investors, market participants, and regulators, it is crucial to comprehend the causes of price volatility and its effects. The development of valuation models, market maturation, and mitigation strategies can all help to create a more secure and robust Bitcoin environment. Individuals may navigate the price volatility of Bitcoin and contribute to the expansion and sustainability of the cryptocurrency industry by accepting the inherent volatility, using risk management, and maintaining a long-term view.

Different approaches to trading Bitcoin

The first decentralized cryptocurrency in the world, Bitcoin, has completely changed the financial industry and given investors access to new and exciting trading options. However, due to Bitcoin's extreme volatility, trading must be done carefully. This section will discuss various trading strategies for Bitcoin, such as day trading, swing trading, and long-term investing. To equip people with the knowledge they need to make wise judgments and successfully traverse the intricacies of Bitcoin trading, we will look into the strategies, methods, and factors related to each strategy.

Day trading is a type of investment that involves purchasing as well as selling an asset within the same trading day in order to profit from small price shifts that occur frequently but only for a short period of time. Technical analysis, scalping strategies, and stop loss orders are used by traders to make quick judgments and lock in winnings. To limit potential losses, day trading requires active monitoring and methodical risk management.

Swing trading targets profits from short- to medium-term trends by concentrating on intermediate-term price fluctuations. To determine entry and exit positions, traders use technical analysis, trend-following strategies, and support and resistance levels. To optimize potential profits, swing trading calls for patience, strict position management, and adherence to a trading strategy.

Holding Bitcoin for longer periods of time is considered long-term investing because of the conviction that its value would increase over time. Long-term investment decisions are guided by fundamental analysis, which includes adoption rates, regulatory developments, and macroeconomic considerations. The HODLing strategy and dollar-cost averaging reduce short-term price volatility while maximizing Bitcoin's long-term utility.

According to the state of the market, many traders use hybrid strategies, integrating components from several systems. When selecting a strategy, risk assessment and reward evaluation are crucial factors to take into account because higher-risk approaches may produce bigger profits but also expose traders to significant losses. Success in the competitive Bitcoin business requires constant learning, staying current on industry developments, and being adaptable.

There are several ways to trade Bitcoin, and each one has its own set of concerns, strategies, and techniques. Swing trading catches intermediate trends, whereas day trading lets you profit from short-term price changes. Investing for the long run concentrates on Bitcoin's potential future value growth. When choosing their preferred strategy, traders must take into account aspects like time commitment, risk management, market analysis, and emotional control. The key to overcoming the complexity of Bitcoin trading is to combine strategies and to continuously learn and adapt. Individuals can make knowledgeable selections and confidently participate in the dynamic world of Bitcoin trading by comprehending the various ways and the accompanying techniques and concerns.

Long-term investing strategies

A digital currency with substantial long-term investment potential has emerged: Bitcoin. Even if short-term trading can be profitable, pursuing a long-term investment strategy enables people to benefit from Bitcoin's future growth and secure a share in the developing cryptocurrency market. This section will examine various long-term Bitcoin investing techniques, highlighting their advantages, factors to consider, and potential concerns. Investors may negotiate the Bitcoin market's volatile environment and put themselves in a position for long-term success by being aware of these strategies.

Holding an investment asset for a long time while putting less emphasis on short-term price swings and more on the asset's potential for overall growth. It involves taking into account elements that affect Bitcoin's long-term viability, including as market trends, fundamental analysis, technological advancements, adoption rates, and legislative changes.

Individuals should perform fundamental analysis and study on Bitcoin in order to make educated investment selections. This analysis involves assessing Bitcoin's underlying principles, including its technology, community, adoption rates, and potential use cases. Investors can evaluate the long-term viability and growth potential of Bitcoin as an investment asset by being aware of these variables. Gaining knowledge about Bitcoin's future possibilities also requires research into market patterns, investor attitude, regulatory changes, and macroeconomic issues.

A well-liked long-term investing method that lessens the impact of short-term price changes is dollar-cost averaging (DCA). It entails consistently investing a specific sum of money in Bitcoin at predetermined intervals, regardless of the price on the open market. Investors can accumulate Bitcoin over time and profit from the potential development of the asset by sticking to a regular investing schedule. However, while employing DCA as a long-term investment strategy, investors should take into account transaction costs, time, and the general direction of Bitcoin's price.

Regardless of short-term price swings, the buy and hold approach comprises buying Bitcoin with the purpose of holding it for a long time. This strategy is predicated on the conviction that Bitcoin has the potential for long-term growth and can outperform conventional investment assets. Investors can reduce transaction costs, make simpler investment decisions, and gain from Bitcoin's potential long-term growth by using a buy and hold strategy. Investors must, however, carefully consider the long-term prospects of Bitcoin, manage any dangers, and keep a close eye on market events.

Any long-term investment strategy, including Bitcoin, must include diversification. Investors can lower the risk involved with any one investment by spreading their investments over a variety of asset classes. Bitcoin diversification reduces total risk while giving access to its future growth. Risk management procedures must include routine portfolio reviews, risk assessments, and holdings rebalancing. Investors can successfully control negative risks and protect money by maintaining the correct asset allocation.

Patience and emotional fortitude are necessary for long-term investing. The volatile character of Bitcoin and market changes can put investors' resolve to the test. People who want to succeed need to keep a long-term perspective, concentrate on the fundamentals, and refrain from acting emotionally in response to short-term market fluctuations. Investors can withstand market downturns and avoid impulsive moves that might impede long-term financial performance by remaining patient and resilient.

Financial advisors who focus on cryptocurrency investing may be of assistance to investors. These consultants can offer insightful advice and support in coordinating long-term investment plans with monetary objectives, risk tolerance, and total investment portfolios. When choosing investing platforms, custodial services, and Bitcoin-related products, extensive due research is also essential. Risks linked with investing in Bitcoin can be reduced by doing research on reliable exchanges, comprehending security measures, and taking regulatory compliance into account.

Long-term Bitcoin investment plans give people the chance to profit from potential growth and secure a share in the developing cryptocurrency sector. Investors can set themselves up for long-term success by engaging in basic study, adopting methods like dollar-cost averaging and buy and hold, diversifying their portfolios, minimizing risks, remaining patient, and obtaining professional assistance. While investing in Bitcoin entails certain risks, with careful thought, research, and a disciplined approach, one may successfully navigate the ever-changing cryptocurrency investment landscape and realize Bitcoin's long-term potential as a valued asset class. Individuals can take part in the ongoing digital revolution and possibly profit from Bitcoin's continued growth and adoption by adopting a long-term investing attitude.

Managing risks and avoiding common pitfalls

The world of digital finance is full of interesting potential for investment in Bitcoin. It's crucial to understand, though, that enormous promise also has inherent risks. This section will examine several risk management techniques and common Bitcoin investment problems. Investors may protect their Bitcoin investments and navigate the dynamic and occasionally volatile character of the cryptocurrency market by putting good risk management measures into place and remaining vigilant.

Investments in bitcoin have certain risks that should be carefully considered. The market's volatility and price changes are what make Bitcoin unique. Investors must be willing to assume the inherent risk brought on by these price fluctuations. Additionally, investors are vulnerable to market manipulation and fraudulent activities due to the unregulated structure of the cryptocurrency market, therefore caution and monitoring are required.

Making informed decisions is essential to managing risks successfully. Investors should undertake extensive background research on Bitcoin, comprehending its technology, community, adoption rates, and potential threats. It's important to keep up with the most recent innovations, legislative changes, and industry trends. To find reputable projects and prevent frauds, it's essential to perform due diligence on potential investment opportunities, such as initial coin offerings (ICOs) or altcoins.

It is crucial to establish investment goals based on individual financial goals and time horizons. The right investment strategy is determined by matching investment goals with risk tolerance, whether the aim is long-term growth, capital preservation, or wealth expansion. Investors can choose strategies that correspond to their comfort levels by evaluating their risk tolerance while taking into account aspects such as financial stability, investment experience, and emotional resilience.

For any portfolio of investments, including Bitcoin, diversification is a crucial risk management strategy. The risks associated with any one investment can be reduced by diversifying assets across other asset classes, including Bitcoin and conventional investments. Diversification raises the possibility of stable returns while reducing exposure to the volatility of a single asset. It is important to take market conditions, risk tolerance, and investing goals into account when choosing the right asset allocation.

Investors should use risk management techniques that are specific to their investment profiles in order to properly control risks. Investors can minimize their potential losses during market downturns by using stop-loss orders to define specified price levels at which they would sell their Bitcoin holdings. Maintaining the target asset allocation and adjusting to shifting market conditions are made easier by routinely evaluating and rebalancing investment portfolios.

It is essential to protect your Bitcoin holdings from theft and hackers. Important security precautions include implementing secure wallets, utilizing multi-factor authentication, and keeping backup copies of wallet data. Protection is increased by following recommended procedures for online security, such as creating strong passwords, enabling two-factor authentication, and being watchful for phishing attempts. Software updates on a regular basis and knowledge of current cybersecurity issues add another layer of protection.

Effective risk management requires constant monitoring of market trends, legislative developments, and industry news. To make wise selections, investors should read reliable news sources, interact with the Bitcoin community, and keep an eye on market indications. Avoiding impulsive decisions prompted by short-term price swings requires emotional discipline and patience.

Financial advisors who focus on cryptocurrency investing should be consulted for insightful advice. Expert consultants offer industry insights, aid with risk profile assessment, and create individualized risk management plans. Discussions with seasoned investors, participation in forums, and interaction with the Bitcoin community all promote mutual learning and support.

Successful Bitcoin investments depend on managing risks and avoiding typical mistakes. Investors can protect their Bitcoin investments and navigate the dynamic cryptocurrency market with more confidence by conducting thorough research, setting clear investment goals, diversifying portfolios, implementing risk management strategies, giving priority to security measures, staying informed, and seeking professional advice. People can maximize the benefits of Bitcoin while limiting any potential drawbacks by using wise and diligent methods. Investors may position themselves for long-term success in the fascinating world of Bitcoin investments by taking a proactive approach to risk management.

CHAPTER VII
Bitcoin Regulation and Legal Considerations

Overview of Bitcoin regulations worldwide

The first cryptocurrency, Bitcoin, has revolutionized traditional finance and is now widely used throughout the world. Due to the fact that Bitcoin is a digital currency that operates internationally, governments and regulatory agencies all around the world have created frameworks to control its usage. This section will give a global overview of Bitcoin laws and explore the various stances that various nations and areas have taken. We will look at the rationale behind regulatory actions, the essential elements of regulatory frameworks, as well as the challenges and opportunities they present. Individuals and companies may negotiate the complexity of Bitcoin transactions with confidence and compliance by being aware of the changing regulatory landscape.

By tackling threats like fraud, hacking, and Ponzi schemes connected to Bitcoin and other cryptocurrencies, regulators seek to protect consumers. Regulations help safeguard consumers from potential losses and boost trust in the exchange of digital assets.

Because Bitcoin is pseudonymous, there are questions regarding how it might be used for illegal purposes. By enforcing Anti-Money Laundering (AML) and Counter-Terrorist financing (CTF) restrictions on Bitcoin exchanges and service providers, regulators aim to prevent money laundering, terrorist financing, and other illicit activity.

Regulators are keeping an eye on the risks posed by Bitcoin in order to ensure financial stability given the cryptocurrency's potential influence on conventional banking institutions. They might decide to implement regulations in order to combat systemic risks, market manipulation, and excessive speculation.

Some nations have made the decision to forbid or severely limit the use of Bitcoin and other cryptocurrencies. Prohibition may be a response to worries about capital flight, a lack of financial system regulation, or a perception of hazards to national security. Outright ban, however, can promote shadow economies and hinder innovation.

Numerous jurisdictions have chosen to treat Bitcoin as a digital asset or commodity and to give it legal recognition. This strategy accepts the reality of cryptocurrencies while subjecting them to certain laws like taxation, consumer protection, and anti-money laundering procedures.

Regulators in numerous nations demand that Bitcoin exchanges and service providers register with the appropriate authorities or get licenses. These steps are intended to guarantee adherence to legal requirements, encourage transparency, and lessen dangers related to the cryptocurrency ecosystem.

Some nations have created regulatory "sandboxes" that let entrepreneurs and companies in the cryptocurrency sector operate with more relaxed regulations. Sandboxes offer a controlled setting for innovation and experimentation while upholding consumer protection and reducing risks.

Know Your Customer (KYC) and AML requirements are frequently placed on Bitcoin exchanges and service providers by regulations. Verifying customer identities and putting policies in place to prevent money laundering and terrorism financing are two of these needs.

Specific licensing or registration requirements for Bitcoin-related firms may be outlined in regulatory frameworks. These processes entail meeting particular requirements, proving compliance with legal requirements, and upholding operational openness.

The taxation of Bitcoin and other cryptocurrencies is now a topic of discussion among governments all over the world. Cryptocurrencies may be treated as assets subject to capital gains tax, transactional VAT, or other tax responsibilities under tax legislation.

Regulators may impose reporting and disclosure requirements on Bitcoin exchanges and service providers. These commitments include disclosing transaction information, delivering consistent financial reports, and participating in regulatory audits.

There are various approaches and interpretations among nations, creating a fragmented worldwide regulatory environment for Bitcoin. This fragmentation presents difficulties for multinational corporations and might prevent Bitcoin from integrating smoothly into the world financial system.

The problem for regulators is to keep up with the quickly advancing technology in the cryptocurrency industry. It takes a thorough understanding of the technology and its potential implications to strike a balance between promoting innovation and safeguarding customers.

Due to Bitcoin's global character, regulatory issues must be successfully resolved through international regulatory collaboration. Sharing best practices, harmonizing laws, and creating uniform frameworks can all be facilitated through collaboration.

As governments and regulatory agencies struggle with the benefits and problems posed by cryptocurrencies, Bitcoin regulations around the world continue to change. Although there are many reasons for regulation, from financial stability to consumer protection, the methods used by various countries varies greatly. For individuals and organizations conducting Bitcoin transactions, it is crucial to comprehend the fundamental elements of regulatory frameworks, including KYC and AML regulations, licensing procedures, taxation, and reporting requirements. It's critical to keep up with regulatory changes in certain jurisdictions and, when needed, seek legal and compliance guidance. Individuals and organizations can make use of the promise of Bitcoin while ensuring compliance with regional laws and international standards by navigating the ever-changing regulatory landscape with awareness, adaptation, and compliance.

Tax implications of Bitcoin transactions

The first cryptocurrency, Bitcoin, has revolutionized the financial world by providing users with a decentralized and international digital currency. The tax implications of using Bitcoin must be understood, though, as it becomes more and more popular. The tax implications and considerations of Bitcoin transactions will be discussed in this section. Key topics such income tax, capital gains tax, reporting requirements, and foreign taxation will be covered in depth. Individuals and organizations may manage the complexity of taxes and guarantee compliance with relevant tax regulations by getting a thorough awareness of the tax environment surrounding Bitcoin.

Bitcoin and other cryptocurrencies are typically treated as property rather than currency by tax authorities around the world. This classification has important tax implications because it calls for people to report gains or losses from Bitcoin transactions.

Buying or selling Bitcoin for fiat money, trading Bitcoin for goods or services, getting Bitcoin as payment, mining Bitcoin, and other Bitcoin transactions all have the potential to result in taxable events. Depending on the tax regulations of the relevant jurisdiction, each event could have a different impact on taxes.

Income tax is applicable to Bitcoin mining profits. The worth of each Bitcoin that was mined must be reported by miners as taxable income at the time of receipt. In addition, many mining-related costs, including those for power and equipment, may be tax deductible.

Bitcoin is regarded as taxable income when it is used as payment for goods or services. For taxation purposes, the recipient must include the fair market value of the Bitcoin they received at the time of the transaction in their income.

Taxes on capital gains apply to any gains or losses from buying and selling Bitcoin. The holding time and the purpose of the transaction both influence the tax treatment. For Bitcoin held for less than a year, short-term capital gains are normally taxed at greater rates than long-term capital gains, which enjoy lower tax rates.

Calculating capital gains or losses requires knowing the cost basis of Bitcoin. It is crucial to maintain accurate records, including proof of the dates, costs, and fees associated with purchases. The cost basis can be established in a number of ways, including FIFO (First-In-First-Out) or particular identification.

Tax authorities demand that people register Bitcoin transactions that exceed a particular amount. The value of Bitcoin kept at the conclusion of the tax year, as well as the sale of Bitcoin and Bitcoin received in payment, must all be reported.

Bitcoin exchanges and payment processors in the US are required to provide Form 1099-K to customers who reach certain transaction criteria. The gross amount of Bitcoin transactions is reported on Form 1099-K, providing data that must be reported on the taxpayer's tax return.

The fact that Bitcoin has no geographical boundaries makes it difficult for tax officials to ascertain the relevant tax regulations. When conducting cross-border Bitcoin transactions, individuals must take into account the tax implications in both their home jurisdiction and the counterparty's jurisdiction.

Tax treaties between nations may have an effect on how Bitcoin transactions are taxed by defining how taxing authority should be distributed and possibly preventing double taxation. Additionally, when doing international Bitcoin transactions, people might be subject to reporting requirements like the Common Reporting Standard (CRS) or Foreign Bank Account Reports (FBAR).

Given the complexity of Bitcoin taxation, consulting with tax experts who are also knowledgeable about cryptocurrencies is strongly advised. Understanding precise tax requirements, optimizing allowable deductions, and maintaining compliance with tax rules are all made easier with the help of tax professionals.

For tax compliance, it's essential to keep detailed records of all Bitcoin transactions, including purchase and sell invoices, transaction summaries, and cost basis data. Maintaining accurate records can make filing taxes easier and support any claims or deductions.

Understanding the tax implications of Bitcoin transactions is crucial for both individuals and businesses as the cryptocurrency gains popularity. The property status of Bitcoin and its wide spectrum of taxable events complicate tax planning and reporting. It is important to properly negotiate issues including income tax on bitcoin mining and payment, capital gains tax on purchasing and selling Bitcoin, reporting obligations, and global tax implications. Effective management of Bitcoin tax liabilities requires seeking professional advice, keeping detailed records, and making sure that all applicable tax laws are followed. Individuals and organizations can comfortably engage in Bitcoin transactions while satisfying their tax obligations and leveraging the advantages of digital currency ownership by comprehending the tax landscape and implementing appropriate tax procedures.

Legal challenges and controversies surrounding Bitcoin

The first decentralized digital currency in the world, Bitcoin, has transformed the financial industry and attracted considerable media interest. Bitcoin, however, encounters a number of legal challenges and controversies as it continues to grow in popularity. We will explore the legal complications of Bitcoin in this section, including regulatory ambiguity, worries about money laundering, taxation concerns, and its connection to illegal activity. We seek to shed light on the changing legal landscape of Bitcoin and its implications for individuals, businesses, and governments by analyzing these challenges and conflicts.

Due to its distinctive features, governments and regulatory entities find it difficult to categorize Bitcoin. Bitcoin's legal and regulatory position depends on whether it should be treated as a currency, a commodity, or a digital asset.

The different regulatory stances taken toward Bitcoin around the world have left the legal system fragmented. For individuals and businesses that operate across borders, a lack of uniformity presents difficulties, complicating compliance and raising legal questions.

Because Bitcoin is pseudonymous, there are questions regarding how it may be used for illegal activity and money laundering. According to detractors, the anonymity of Bitcoin transactions attracts criminals looking to launder money or conduct illegal transactions.

To combat the risks of cryptocurrency-related money laundering, governments all over the world have put in place Know Your Customer (KYC) and anti-money laundering (AML) regulations. According to these regulations, companies and exchanges must investigate their clients and report any questionable transactions.

There are tax implications if Bitcoin is categorized as property rather than currency. The proper tax treatment, including capital gains tax, income tax on mining, and reporting requirements, is a problem for tax authorities in many jurisdictions.

The decentralized nature of Bitcoin makes it difficult for tax authorities to ascertain the tax implications of international transactions. The complexity of Bitcoin taxation in a worldwide setting is still being addressed through tax treaties and international tax systems.

Legal systems are challenged by legal disputes resulting from Bitcoin transactions, such as contract breaches or fraud. Because of the international nature of Bitcoin transactions, establishing jurisdiction, upholding contracts, and retrieving assets in the event of disputes can be challenging.

Increasingly more regulatory enforcement measures are being taken against deceptive schemes, unregistered exchanges, and non-compliant companies. Although these measures are intended to safeguard consumers and preserve market integrity, they also raise concerns about the boundaries of regulatory power and potential regulatory overreach.

Blockchain, the technology that underpins Bitcoin, has the potential to revolutionize many other industries. However, legal frameworks have found it difficult to keep up with the rapid development of blockchain, leading to concerns about intellectual property rights, data privacy, and the enforceability of smart contracts.

Initial Coin Offerings (ICOs), a kind of fundraising that involves the issue of digital tokens, have come under legal attention because of worries about investor protection and securities legislation. Determining when tokens should be categorized as securities and be subject to current regulatory frameworks has proven difficult for regulators.

Investors are at risk because of the volatility of the price of Bitcoin and the possibility of market manipulation. By encouraging investor awareness and educating the public on the associated risks with investing in cryptocurrencies, governments and authorities aim to protect consumers.

Because Bitcoin is decentralized and largely unregulated, it has fostered an atmosphere that is conducive to fraud and shady business practices. Targeting gullible people, pyramid schemes, phishing scams, and bogus initial coin offerings have surfaced. Public safety depends on educating customers and implementing anti-fraud laws.

The introduction of Bitcoin disrupted established banking structures and caused various legal controversies and challenges. The legal environment surrounding Bitcoin is constantly changing due to regulatory uncertainty, concerns about money laundering and other illegal activity, taxation challenges, legal battles, and investor protection concerns. Finding the right solutions and striking a balance between innovation, consumer protection, and preserving the integrity of financial markets is a challenge for governments, regulators, and legal systems. Policymakers can create strong regulatory frameworks that encourage innovation while preserving the public interest by negotiating these legal issues. To successfully manage the legal environment surrounding Bitcoin, individuals and organizations should be updated about the changing legal requirements, obtain legal counsel as needed, and adhere to compliance duties.

Future prospects for Bitcoin regulation

The revolutionary cryptocurrency Bitcoin has disrupted established financial systems and generated a debate about the necessity of regulatory frameworks on a worldwide scale. The future prospects for Bitcoin regulation continue to be a subject of significant interest as governments and regulatory agencies struggle with the difficulties and opportunities posed by the cryptocurrency. We will explore the implications and possible futures of Bitcoin regulation in this section. We'll talk about important topics like legal frameworks, international cooperation, technological developments, and the evolving role of cryptocurrencies in the world economy. We seek to clarify the future and any potential effects on people, businesses, and the larger financial landscape by looking at these prospects.

The creation of more standard and transparent regulatory frameworks is one potential future opportunity for Bitcoin regulation. Governments and regulatory organizations may strive to establish clear regulations that specify Bitcoin's legal standing, taxation, reporting requirements, and investor safeguards. Regulations that are clear can promote innovation while preventing illegal activity.

Striking a balance between promoting innovation and upholding financial stability is a problem for regulators. Future regulatory frameworks may be designed to handle concerns connected with cryptocurrencies, such as market volatility, systemic hazards, and consumer protection, while fostering an environment that promotes technological innovation.

To address the global nature of Bitcoin, international cooperation among governments and regulatory agencies is crucial. To improve cross-border transactions and lessen regulatory fragmentation, future prospects may involve coordinating regulatory strategies, exchanging best practices, and adopting uniform standards.

Future regulatory efforts might concentrate on improving cross-border enforcement tools when Bitcoin transactions cross national boundaries. Collaboration in combating cryptocurrency-related money laundering, terrorist funding, and other illegal activity can improve regulatory efficiency and promote trust in the global financial system.

Blockchain, the technology that underpins Bitcoin, has enormous promise outside of digital currencies. Future legislation may be geared toward promoting the use of blockchain technology across a range of industries while resolving issues with data privacy, smart contracts, and interoperability.

Governments now have the chance to investigate the integration of Bitcoin and other cryptocurrencies into their monetary systems due to the growth of central bank digital currencies (CBDCs). Regulatory frameworks that support the coexistence of CBDCs and decentralized cryptocurrencies in the future may be necessary to foster financial inclusion and innovation.

Future legislation may concentrate on creating a secure and regulated environment for their participation as institutional investors increasingly enter the Bitcoin market. This might entail the creation of investment frameworks, custodial laws, and infrastructure for institutional-grade Bitcoin trading and storage.

The possible integration of Bitcoin with conventional financial systems may influence future regulatory strategies. Collaboration between cryptocurrency exchanges and established financial institutions may result in more reliable compliance controls, interoperability, and a smooth integration of cryptocurrencies into current frameworks.

Future prospects may see a change in the regulatory approach toward Bitcoin from initial skepticism and resistance to a more cooperative stance. To foster dialogue, comprehend the potential benefits, and proactively address concerns, regulators may actively interact with industry stakeholders, academic institutions, and technology developers.

Future regulation might take into account how people's perceptions of cryptocurrencies are changing as public awareness and comprehension of Bitcoin continue to rise. To educate consumers, combat misinformation, and increase public trust in the potential advantages of Bitcoin and other digital currencies, regulatory actions must be taken.

The prospects for regulating Bitcoin in the future are complex and include legal frameworks, international collaboration, technological developments, and the changing place of cryptocurrencies in the global economy. The future regulatory landscape must be shaped by establishing regulatory uniformity and transparency, balancing innovation and stability, and encouraging global cooperation. Embracing technical developments offers opportunities for integration and wide-scale adoption, such as blockchain technology and digital currencies issued by central banks. Future regulation of Bitcoin should take into account the potential advantages while addressing dangers and guaranteeing consumer protection as the technology continues to develop. Regulators, companies, and individuals can fully utilize the promise of Bitcoin while preserving the integrity and stability of the international financial system by forging ahead with an open and cooperative approach.

CHAPTER
VIII
Alternative Cryptocurrencies
and the Future of Bitcoin

Introduction to other popular cryptocurrencies

While Bitcoin continues to be the most well-known and prominent cryptocurrency, the landscape of digital currencies has dramatically changed, giving rise to other alternative cryptocurrencies. We will address some of the well-known cryptocurrencies that have emerged alongside Bitcoin in this section. We will investigate their special qualities, underlying technologies, and potential uses. We seek to present an overview of the developing digital asset ecosystem and emphasize the potential impact of these alternative cryptocurrencies by delving into the various world of cryptocurrencies.

A decentralized blockchain platform called Ethereum (ETH) facilitates the development and execution of smart contracts. Developers can now create decentralized applications (DApps) and launch new digital assets using initial coin offerings (ICOs) due to the introduction of the idea of programmable money.

The ability to carry out smart contracts, self-executing contracts with predefined circumstances, is what makes Ethereum unique. This functionality has paved the way for numerous decentralized applications in a variety of sectors, including identity management, gambling, banking, and supply chain.

A digital payment protocol called Ripple (XRP) was created to make quick, inexpensive, and secure cross-border transactions possible. A bridge currency for allowing transfers between several fiat currencies is its native cryptocurrency, called XRP.

The architecture and consensus mechanism of Ripple are designed to increase the effectiveness of conventional banking institutions. It may revolutionize international remittances and liquidity management by allowing financial institutions to settle transactions in real-time and at lower rates.

A peer-to-peer cryptocurrency developed by Charlie Lee, Litecoin (LTC) is frequently referred to as the silver to Bitcoin's gold. Despite having a different hashing algorithm and faster block generation times than Bitcoin, it is very comparable to that digital currency.

Litecoin differs from Bitcoin in that its block generation time is faster and its supply limit is higher. It promises to speed up transaction confirmations and give regular consumers a second choice for digital currency.

A blockchain platform called Cardano (ADA) intends to offer a safe and expandable foundation for the creation of decentralized applications and smart contracts. It places a strong emphasis on a blockchain-focused, academically rigorous approach.

Ouroboros, a unique consensus algorithm developed by Cardano, makes use of the proof-of-stake protocol. In contrast to Bitcoin's energy-intensive proof-of-work process, it aims to improve scalability, energy efficiency, and overall sustainability.

A blockchain protocol called Polkadot (DOT) intends to make it possible for several blockchains to communicate with one another seamlessly. It aims to get around scalability issues and promote cooperation across various blockchain networks.

The "web of blockchains" proposed by Polkadot enables the transfer of assets and data between several chains. It provides opportunities for specialized blockchains to collaborate and share assets, ultimately improving the usability and functionality of decentralized applications.

With an emphasis on financial inclusion, Stellar (XLM) is a decentralized platform created to make quick and affordable cross-border payments possible. It aspires to link individuals, payment systems, and financial institutions to build a diverse global financial network.

The representation of multiple assets on the blockchain is made possible by Stellar's network, which enables the seamless issuance and transfer of tokens. This function makes it possible to tokenize physical assets and conduct micropayments and remittances.

Alternative cryptocurrencies offer a variety of features and use cases beyond Bitcoin's pioneering role as the cryptocurrency market continues to develop. The growing ecosystem of digital assets benefits from the capabilities of Ethereum's smart contracts, Ripple's concentration on effective worldwide payments, Litecoin's quick transactions, Cardano's methodical approach, Polkadot's interoperability, Stellar's financial inclusion, and many other cryptocurrencies. Each cryptocurrency targets a different problem and serves a distinct purpose, creating new opportunities for disruption and innovation across numerous industries. Individuals and companies can obtain a deeper grasp of the digital asset ecosystem and take into account the potential effects and opportunities they bring by exploring these alternative cryptocurrencies.

Exploring the potential of blockchain technology beyond Bitcoin

Although blockchain technology was first popularized by Bitcoin, it has many uses that go far beyond just cryptocurrencies. This section will highlight the transformational potential of blockchain technology across a range of industries. We'll look into blockchain's core properties, like decentralization, transparency, immutability, and security. We seek to illuminate the enormous potential of blockchain technology beyond Bitcoin by looking at real-world use cases, difficulties, and future prospects.

By spreading data among numerous nodes and obtaining consensus through consensus techniques like Proof of Work (PoW) or Proof of Stake (PoS), blockchain technology enables decentralized networks. As a result, there is no need for centralized authorities, and participant trust is increased.

All participants may examine and confirm transactions that are recorded on the distributed ledger due to blockchain's transparency. The nearly unchangeable nature of transactions once they are committed to the blockchain improves data security and integrity.

By offering an immutable and transparent record that follows the flow of goods from the point of origin to the final consumer, blockchain can transform supply chain management. This makes it possible to increase supply chain optimization, authenticity verification, and traceability.

By establishing a reliable and impenetrable record of a product's provenance, assuring authenticity, and limiting the circulation of fake items, blockchain technology can help fight fraud and counterfeiting.

Cross-border payments might be streamlined by means of blockchain-based solutions, which would lower costs, speed up transactions, and broaden financial access. Blockchain technology has the power to transform the remittance sector and enable direct peer-to-peer transactions by getting rid of middlemen.

Decentralized finance (DeFi) now has more options due to smart contracts, self-executing agreements stored on the blockchain. Blockchain-based platforms are transforming traditional financial services by enabling the development of decentralized lending, borrowing, and trading systems.

A safe and decentralized foundation for managing health data is provided by blockchain technology. The blockchain can be used to store patient data, conduct medical research, and manage consent while preserving data integrity, privacy, and interoperability.

Pharmaceutical industry problems with drug authentication and supply chains can be solved with blockchain. Blockchain increases transparency, lowers the incidence of fake medications, and enhances patient safety by tracing the movement of drugs across the supply chain.

Voting systems powered by blockchain can improve accountability, decrease fraud, and boost voter trust in the political process. The blockchain's immutable records guarantee the accuracy of vote information and make audits quick and easy.

Blockchain technology can give people control over their personal data and speed up identification verification procedures by giving them self-sovereign digital IDs. This has effects on a number of public services, including the issuance of passports, licenses for drivers, and social services.

Blockchain technology still has scalability issues due to restrictions in network capacity and transaction processing speed. The goal of ongoing research and the creation of novel solutions is to address these problems and open the door for widespread adoption.

Regulatory frameworks must keep up with technological improvements as blockchain applications develop. Governments and regulatory organizations need to strike a balance between fostering innovation and responding to issues with consumer rights, privacy, and data protection.

Blockchain technology offers disruptive opportunities across businesses and goes far beyond Bitcoin. It offers prospects for improved traceability, faster procedures, and increased confidence due to its decentralized nature, transparency, and security. Blockchain is altering established processes and fostering innovation across a range of industries, including supply chain management, finance, healthcare, and government. Despite obstacles, continued research and development as well as legal frameworks will help blockchain reach its full potential. A more inclusive and decentralized future can be achieved by embracing blockchain technology with a forward-thinking mindset, which can open up new doors for efficiency, transparency, and collaboration.

Future developments and current trends in the cryptocurrency space

Since the creation of Bitcoin in 2009, there has been significant expansion and development in the cryptocurrency industry. We will examine current trends and potential future changes in the cryptocurrency sector in this section, highlighting the way forward for innovation. We'll explore important topics including decentralized finance (DeFi), non-fungible tokens (NFTs), central bank digital currencies (CBDCs), scaling solutions, and the possible effects of developing technology. We seek to offer insights into the revolutionary potential of cryptocurrencies and their role in influencing the future of finance and technology by exploring these trends and developments.

Decentralized financial instrument (DeFi) refers to the use of smart contracts and blockchain technology to replicate conventional financial products. It covers borrowing, lending, decentralized exchanges, yield farming, as well as other innovative financial applications.

DeFi has grown rapidly, and there are now several different protocols worth billions of dollars. DeFi provides people with increased financial inclusion, direct access to financial services, and the opportunity for larger returns. However, difficulties including security vulnerabilities and regulatory issues still exist.

Non-Fungible Tokens (NFTs) are special digital tokens that signify ownership or provide proof of authenticity for digital goods like music, artwork, and other things. They make use of blockchain technology to offer verifiability, provenance, and scarcity.

NFTs have revolutionized the arts and entertainment sectors by allowing artists to make money off of their digital works and interact with their audience directly. They provide new sources of income, fractional ownership, and open royalty structures. However, issues with copyright infringement and environmental concerns continue.

Central Bank Digital Currencies (CBDCs) are digital representations of a nation's fiat currency that are created and managed by a central bank. They seek to blend the programmability and efficiency of cryptocurrencies with the stability of conventional fiat currencies.

CBDCs have benefits like increased financial inclusion, higher payment efficiency, and improved monetary policy tools. However, while putting them into practice, it is important to take into account issues with privacy, cybersecurity, and monetary sovereignty.

Scalability issues with blockchain technology exist in terms of network capacity and transaction processing speed. Scalability solutions are essential to provide effective and scalable blockchain networks as the demand for cryptocurrencies rises.

In order to reduce congestion and increase transaction throughput, layer-2 solutions like payment channels and sidechains are used. Communication between various blockchain networks is facilitated through interoperability protocols like Polkadot and Cosmos, increasing scalability and flexibility.

Supply chain management, logistics, and data integrity are just a few industries that could benefit from the combination of blockchain and also Internet of Things (IoT) technologies. IoT ecosystems' security and trust can be improved by blockchain's decentralized and transparent nature.

Data privacy, identity management, and predictive analytics might all be revolutionized by the fusion of blockchain with artificial intelligence (AI). Blockchain can give AI algorithms a safe and verifiable framework, increasing trust and privacy protection.

The regulatory issues presented by cryptocurrencies are being aggressively addressed by governments and regulatory authorities worldwide. To assure investment safety, anti-money laundering compliance, and consumer rights, regulatory frameworks are evolving.

Interoperability standards, security guidelines, and best practices are being developed by standardizing organizations and industry consortiums. Efforts towards standardization can promote cooperation, improve interoperability, and create uniform frameworks for the cryptocurrency industry.

A transformative era in technology and finance is signaled by current trends and future developments in the cryptocurrency space. Key forces behind innovation include DeFi, NFTs, CBDCs, scaling solutions, and future technologies. While there are difficulties, it is impossible to ignore the potential advantages of cryptocurrencies in terms of ownership rights, efficiency, and security. The future of cryptocurrencies will be shaped by stakeholder collaboration, legislative clarity, and technological developments, paving the path for a more decentralized, inclusive, and effective global financial system. Embracing the potential of these trends and developments can open up new opportunities and spark good change as the cryptocurrency industry continues to flourish.

Predictions and possibilities for the future of Bitcoin

Since its inception, Bitcoin, the original cryptocurrency, has completely altered the financial landscape. It is only reasonable to make predictions about Bitcoin's trajectory and potential effects as it continues to gain popularity. The future of Bitcoin will be predicted and discussed in this section, taking into account important elements including acceptance, regulation, technological development, macroeconomic trends, and sociological changes. We want to offer insights into the possible directions that Bitcoin may take and its transformative potential by evaluating these characteristics.

The growing involvement of institutional investors in the cryptocurrency market is a sign of Bitcoin's expanding potential and acceptance. Major corporations, hedge funds, and asset managers could make investments that increase market liquidity, stability, and acceptance.

It's possible that Bitcoin will gradually replace traditional currencies for everyday transactions as more shops and services start to accept it as payment. Wider adoption and use of Bitcoin can be facilitated by the incorporation of payment gateways for it and the creation of user-friendly wallets.

Regulations governing cryptocurrencies are constantly changing. Businesses and investors may accept Bitcoin more widely and integrate it into conventional financial institutions if regulations are clear and friendly to it.

The potential for central banks to issue virtual money or work with already-existing cryptocurrencies like Bitcoin may help close the gap between centralized fiat currencies and decentralized digital currencies. Increased efficiency, financial inclusion, and stability can result from this integration.

By enabling quicker and less expensive transactions off-chain while employing the security of the underlying blockchain, layer-2 technologies like the Lightning Network can alleviate Bitcoin's scalability issues.

The introduction of confidential transactions or zero-knowledge proofs, for example, are technological advancements targeted at strengthening privacy characteristics inside the Bitcoin network. These advancements may strengthen user privacy and boost adoption among privacy-conscious people and organizations.

Due to its scarcity and decentralized structure, Bitcoin has the potential to act as a hedge against inflation and other economic risks. As the world's financial systems suffer difficulties, Bitcoin might be seen as a store of value more and more, luring investors looking for a virtual substitute for conventional assets.

Bitcoin can offer a decentralized and accessible alternative in nations with unstable currencies or restricted access to conventional banking services. The use of Bitcoin may increase globally and change financial inclusion as a result of increased popularity in emerging markets.

The promise of Bitcoin as a dependable, decentralized digital asset may become increasingly obvious as digital transformation spreads across industries. Economic crises can erode public trust in established financial systems, increasing demand for alternative financial alternatives.

The perception and adoption of cryptocurrencies like Bitcoin can be impacted by geopolitical unrest and currency conflicts. As a borderless and censorship-resistant digital asset, Bitcoin may become more popular in areas where people want to exercise their financial independence or get around capital regulations.

The attention may shift to addressing issues like energy use that are related to bitcoin mining. The Bitcoin network's viability can be improved by continuing to adopt renewable energy sources and creating more energy-efficient mining techniques.

There may be initiatives to promote carbon neutrality and reduce Bitcoin's environmental impact. The network can be brought into line with sustainable practices by the incorporation of carbon credits or the funding of eco-friendly projects using Bitcoin-based methods.

The potential for Bitcoin's future to change the world is vast. As adoption increases, legal frameworks change, new technologies are developed, and public views change, Bitcoin may end up playing a bigger role in the world's financial system. Its function as a medium of exchange, store of value, and decentralized asset class has the potential to transform conventional finance, expand financial inclusion, and stimulate innovation. Bitcoin's resiliency, technological underpinnings, and expanding community give a strong platform for its continued growth and evolution even though difficulties and uncertainties still exist. Bitcoin has the ability to pave the way for a digital future that empowers people, encourages financial independence, and opens up new avenues for economic progress by embracing the possibilities and solving the problems.

CONCLUSION

Recap of key points covered in the e-book

Throughout the course of this e-book, we have explored a variety of aspects of Bitcoin, including its foundations, its historical history, its technological underpinnings, its practical applications, and the regulatory concerns that surround it. In this section, we will review the most important topics discussed in the e-book, providing a concise summary of the most important takeaways and insights obtained from our investigation of the Bitcoin environment. The purpose of this section is to provide a comprehensive overview and to reinforce the knowledge learned throughout the rest of the e-book by reviewing some essential issues.

I. Understanding Bitcoin:

To start, we delved into the fundamentals of Bitcoin, covering topics like as its decentralized nature, the idea behind blockchain technology, and the function of cryptography in ensuring the safety of Bitcoin transactions. We examined the possibilities of Bitcoin both as a medium of trade and as a way to store value, highlighting the ways in which Bitcoin transactions are distinct from those involving traditional currencies.

II. Exploring Bitcoin's History:

We went on a journey through the history of Bitcoin, beginning with its mysterious origins with the publishing of the Bitcoin whitepaper by Satoshi Nakamoto and progressing through its rapid expansion, market swings, and acknowledgment by the mainstream. We talked about significant milestones, important events, and influential figures that played a role in Bitcoin's evolution and popularity during the course of its existence.

III. Key Concepts: Blockchain, Decentralization, and Cryptography:

We went over some of the key ideas of Bitcoin, such as the blockchain, decentralization, and cryptography. We went over how the blockchain can be thought of as a decentralized ledger that not only records all Bitcoin transactions but also ensures their transparency, immutability, and security. In addition to this, we talked about the advantages and disadvantages of decentralization, as well as the crucial part that cryptographic methods play in ensuring the safety of Bitcoin transactions.

IV. How Bitcoin Differs from Traditional Currencies:

In this part, we compared Bitcoin to traditional fiat currencies and emphasized the most important differences between the two. We talked about how Bitcoin is decentralized, how its supply is limited, and how it is independent of central banks and government authority. The consequences of Bitcoin's volatility, transaction speed, and potential for financial inclusion and borderless transactions were also investigated in this part of the e-book.

V. Setting Up a Bitcoin Wallet:

We offered instructions on how to create a Bitcoin wallet, during which we discussed the various wallet options that are currently accessible, such as software wallets, hardware wallets, and online wallets. When it comes to safeguarding one's Bitcoin holdings, we underlined the significance of taking precautions such as using complex passwords, two-factor authentication, and performing regular backups.

VI. Choosing a Reputable Bitcoin Exchange:

Choosing a trustworthy Bitcoin exchange requires careful consideration, and we went through some of the finest methods for doing so. We investigated aspects such as trading fees, liquidity, customer service, and regulatory compliance, as well as user experience, and security measures. Before deciding on an exchange, we highlighted how important it is to first carry out exhaustive study and exercise proper diligence.

VII. Securing Your Bitcoin Holdings:

We investigated the most effective methods of protection against fraud, theft, and hacking since we were aware of the necessity of ensuring the safety of Bitcoin holdings. We talked about other solutions, like as cold storage, wallets that require multiple signatures, and using hardware wallets. In addition to this, we emphasized the significance of always using the most recent versions of software and equipment, remaining vigilant against phishing attempts, and engaging in strict security procedures.

VIII. Buying Your First Bitcoin:

We have published a detailed guide on how to buy Bitcoin, in which we address several options including peer-to-peer exchanges, centralized exchanges, and Bitcoin ATMs. We stressed how important it is to conduct transactions on platforms that have a good reputation, use methods of payment that are secure, and be aware of the potential hazards and volatility in the market.

IX. Exploring Different Types of Bitcoin Wallets:

We went into greater detail regarding the many different kinds of Bitcoin wallets, which include mobile wallets, paper wallets, hardware wallets, and also software wallets. We explored their features, advantages, and considerations, with the goal of assisting readers in selecting the wallet choice that best meets their requirements, ease of use preferences, and preferred levels of security.

X. Understanding Bitcoin Addresses and Private Keys:

We explained how Bitcoin addresses and private keys are generated, kept, and utilized in Bitcoin transactions, thus removing some of the mystery around them. Because they are the means through which Bitcoin holdings may be controlled and accessed, we emphasized the need of keeping private keys secure. We talked about how important it is to safely store private keys, as well as how to make use of mnemonic phrases and different backup solutions.

XI. Using Bitcoin for Transactions:

We explored the practical issues of utilizing Bitcoin for transactions and talked about the process of sending and receiving Bitcoin payments as part of our research. We discussed the function of transaction fees, the significance of validating transaction data, and the significance of using QR codes to streamline the process of making a payment. In addition to this, we discussed the possible advantages of using Bitcoin for international business and online shopping.

XII. Sending and Receiving Bitcoin Payments:

We offered a complete explanation of the steps involved in sending and receiving payments using Bitcoin, emphasizing the necessity of precise recipient addresses, transaction confirmations, and wallet synchronization throughout our discussion. We also explored potential solutions for the scalability of transactions and discussed about the role that transaction fees play in making sure that confirmations are sent out on time.

XIII. How Bitcoin Mining Works:

We removed some of the mystery around the Bitcoin mining process by elaborating on the part that miners play in maintaining the integrity of the network and confirming transactions. During the course of the discussion, we covered the method of solving computational puzzles, the benefits for mining, and the idea of mining pools. We also brought attention to the amount of energy that is consumed by mining and the ongoing efforts that are being made to establish more environmentally friendly mining processes.

XIV. Mining Hardware and Software Options:

We went over the different hardware and software options that are available for mining Bitcoin, and we talked about how mining equipment has progressed from general-purpose CPUs to specialized ASIC miners. We discussed the significance of computing the profitability of mining by taking into account a variety of criteria, including the mining difficulty, the cost of power, and the performance of the mining hardware. We also talked about the various mining software solutions and their importance in terms of making mining operations more efficient.

XV. Joining a Mining Pool:

We discussed about the advantages and things to think about before joining a mining pool. An organization of miners known as a mining pool cooperates to increase the likelihood that they will successfully mine a block and divide the rewards. We looked into the various forms of mining pools, the fees associated with each, and the criteria that should be considered while selecting a pool. We stressed how important it was to do research on the reputation of the pool, the durability of the network, and the payout processes.

XVI. The Role of the Blockchain in Securing Bitcoin Transactions:

We brought attention to the fundamental part that the blockchain plays in the process of protecting Bitcoin transactions by offering a decentralized and unchangeable record of all Bitcoin transactions. We went over the various consensus techniques, including as proof of work and proof of stake, that are responsible for ensuring the legitimacy of transactions and the safety of networks. We also looked into the ways in which blockchain technology could be used for purposes other than Bitcoin.

XVII. Best Practices for Securing Your Bitcoin:

We provided in-depth guidance on the most effective methods for securing Bitcoin holdings, which included recommendations for the creation of robust passwords, the implementation of two-factor authentication, the utilization of multisignature wallets, and the routine update of software and firmware. We underlined the significance of offline storage as well as choices for safe backups as a risk mitigation strategy.

XVIII. Protecting Against Hacks and Scams:

We had a discussion on different ways to protect ourselves from the hazards that are posed by hackers and scams in the cryptocurrency field because we are aware of these dangers. We discussed the significance of maintaining good cybersecurity hygiene, being aware of phishing attempts, and remaining vigilant against fraudulent schemes. When it comes to activities that are related to cryptocurrencies, we also provide guidance on how to recognize trustworthy sites and how to perform thorough research.

XIX. Privacy Considerations When Using Bitcoin:

We discussed the pseudonymous nature of Bitcoin transactions and potential privacy-enhancing approaches such as currency mixing and the usage of privacy-focused wallets as part of our exploration into the privacy implications of using Bitcoin. We investigated the trade-offs that can be made between privacy and regulatory compliance, with a focus on the significance of being aware of the privacy implications that come with using cryptocurrencies like Bitcoin.

XX. Anonymity Versus Transparency in the Bitcoin Network:

We delved into the tension that exists in the Bitcoin network between anonymity and transparency, discussing the pseudonymous nature of transactions as well as the possibility that blockchain analysis could reveal patterns in transaction behavior. We investigated the difficulties and concerns that are associated with privacy, legislation, and the requirement for openness in a number of different use cases.

XXI. Understanding Bitcoin Price Volatility:

We explored the elements that contribute to the price volatility of Bitcoin, such as changes in market demand and investor sentiment, as well as movements in macroeconomic and regulatory policies. We examined the potential risks and opportunities associated with price volatility, and we underlined the need of risk management and long-term investing strategies.

XXII. Different Approaches to Trading Bitcoin:

We looked into a variety of ways to trade Bitcoin, including day trading, swing trading, and investing for the long term. We went over the significance of risk management, technical analysis, and fundamental analysis when it comes to the process of making educated decisions about trading. In addition to this, we underlined how important it is to be aware of the tendencies of the market, to have reasonable expectations, and to devise a trading plan that is methodical.

XXIII. Long-Term Investing Strategies:

We discussed long-term investment ideas for Bitcoin, with a focus on the significance of maintaining a diverse portfolio, utilizing dollar-cost averaging, and having a fundamental knowledge of Bitcoin's value proposition. We talked about the potential advantages and things to think about when making a long-term investment in Bitcoin as a way to protect one's wealth from the effects of inflation.

XXIV. Managing Risks and Avoiding Common Pitfalls:

When working with Bitcoin, we emphasized how important it is to properly manage risks and steer clear of typical errors. We talked about how important it is to undertake extensive research, to have a solid understanding of the mechanics of the market, and to avoid making speculative investments and falling for scams. In addition, we discussed the necessity of staying aware and educated as well as the risk reduction techniques that can be utilized.

XXV. Overview of Bitcoin Regulations Worldwide:

We discussed the differing tactics taken by various nations and jurisdictions as we investigated the global regulatory landscape surrounding Bitcoin. We brought attention to the importance of regulatory clarity, investor safety, and efforts to combat money laundering. When engaging in activities that are related to Bitcoin, we underlined how important it is to ensure that you are always in compliance with the local rules.

XXVI. Tax Implications of Bitcoin Transactions:

We provided an overview of the tax implications of Bitcoin transactions, including topics such as the tax on capital gains, the requirements for filing reports, and the difficulties connected with keeping track of transactions. We highlighted how important it is to get in touch with tax professionals in order to guarantee that one is in compliance with the tax legislation that are in place in each country.

XXVII. Legal Challenges and Controversies Surrounding Bitcoin:

The regulatory ambiguities, political crackdowns, and legal conflicts that surround Bitcoin were investigated, as were the legal problems and controversies surrounding Bitcoin. We talked about the potential influence on the adoption of Bitcoin as well as the requirement for continued legislative frameworks that strike a balance between innovation and consumer protection.

XXVIII. Future Prospects for Bitcoin Regulation:

We took into consideration the changing regulatory landscape, international cooperation, and the incorporation of digital currencies into traditional financial systems as we analyzed the future prospects for Bitcoin regulation. While admitting the difficulties of striking the ideal balance between innovation and stability, we talked about the potential advantages of regulatory transparency and collaboration.

In this e-book, we set out on a tour around the landscape of Bitcoin, investigating its history, core principles, practical usage, regulatory implications, and future prospects. We hope that by providing a summary of the most important aspects discussed, we have not only provided the audience with a good understanding of Bitcoin, but also equipped them with the knowledge and tools necessary to effectively traverse the world of cryptocurrencies. As Bitcoin and the cryptocurrency sector continue to develop, it will be vital for individuals and organizations to stay informed, practice basic security measures, and adapt to changes in legislative regulations in order to harness the revolutionary potential of this ground-breaking technology.

Encouragement for readers to continue learning about Bitcoin

Throughout the course of this e-book, we have investigated the diverse world of Bitcoin, looking into its history as well as its technological foundations, practical applications, and regulatory concerns. As we get to the end of our journey, it is essential to highlight the significance of continuous education and involvement in the ever-evolving world of cryptocurrency. In this section, we will encourage and direct readers to continue their educational discovery of Bitcoin by showcasing the transformative potential, personal growth, and exciting possibilities that await people who embrace this revolutionary technology.

A paradigm shift in both the world of finance and the world of technology has been brought about by Bitcoin. Individuals are able to obtain financial sovereignty, challenge established power systems, and contribute to a global economy that is more inclusive and equitable when they embrace the decentralized nature, transparency, and security of cryptocurrencies. A driver for one's own development as well as a contributor to a more desirable future is the realization that Bitcoin has the ability to disrupt entire sectors, encourage innovation, and give people more control over their own lives.

The Bitcoin market is highly dynamic and constantly evolving. The reader is able to actively engage in the ongoing evolution of Bitcoin so long as they keep themselves updated about the most recent developments, new trends, and regulatory changes. By participating in credible news sources, industry forums, and educational platforms, one can gain insightful knowledge and create a deeper grasp of the complexities and nuances of the Bitcoin setting.

Bitcoin is founded on innovative technology, and its success will depend on the continued development of blockchain technology, cryptography, and decentralized system architecture. They'll be able to stay abreast of developments and understand the full potential of Bitcoin's technological underpinnings if they are encouraged to investigate upcoming technologies such as layer-2 solutions, privacy advancements, and interoperability protocols. This can be accomplished by encouraging readers to study such technologies.

The influence of Bitcoin is not limited to the sphere of money. Its underlying blockchain technology has the capability to revolutionize a variety of different sectors, including healthcare, voting systems, identity verification, and the management of supply chains. Readers can better comprehend the transformative possibilities and chances for innovation and disruption in their respective sectors by delving deeper into these applications.

Education on Bitcoin, along with financial literacy and sound security measures, should go hand in hand. Not only does encouraging readers to further their grasp of personal finance, investing techniques, risk management, and cybersecurity improve their ability to navigate the Bitcoin landscape, but it also encourages responsible and secure participation in the broader cryptocurrency ecosystem.

Developers, business people, cryptocurrency enthusiasts, and scholars all make up the Bitcoin community, which is a thriving and varied ecosystem. In order to develop chances for collaboration, knowledge exchange, and networking, it is important to encourage readers to actively participate in this community. Participating in online forums, going to in-person conferences, and becoming a member of local meeting groups all contribute to the creation of a sense of belonging while also providing opportunities for personal and professional advancement.

The development of Bitcoin is still in its infancy, which means that there is a virtually infinite scope for innovation. The investigation of new concepts, projects, and use cases is made possible by encouraging readers to engage in critical thinking, to challenge established norms, and to investigate potential pathways for experimentation. Readers have the ability to actively contribute to the continued growth and widespread adoption of Bitcoin if they encourage a mindset of curiosity and creativity in themselves.

The effects of Bitcoin become more apparent over time, and it may be years, or even decades, before we completely understand its actual potential. Patience, resilience, and the ability to weather market volatility and regulatory hurdles are all traits that can be fostered by encouraging readers to adopt a long-term perspective. It is important to emphasize the necessity of maintaining a consistent commitment to learning, adapting, and changing in order to guarantee that readers continue to be active participants in Bitcoin's transformational journey.

Bitcoin is a phenomenon that spans international borders and is unaffected by cultural norms because it operates on a decentralized network. A global perspective can be fostered by encouraging readers to investigate the impact Bitcoin has produced in a variety of areas and to gain an understanding of the myriad of difficulties and opportunities it brings. Readers develop a more holistic comprehension of Bitcoin's influence around the globe when they interact with people coming from a variety of cultural and socioeconomic contexts and obtain knowledge about local efforts and developments.

As we get to the end of this e-book, we would want to encourage readers to continue their own personal educational journeys and investigate Bitcoin further. Readers may put themselves at the forefront of this groundbreaking technology by maintaining a mindset that is open to new information, actively participating in the Bitcoin community, and embracing constant learning. Bitcoin has a tremendous opportunity to disrupt entire businesses, give individuals more agency, and broaden access to financial services. Readers have the chance to contribute to a future that is decentralized and equal, fuel their own personal growth, and unleash exciting opportunities for innovation and impact if they actively participate in the Bitcoin ecosystem. The information that you have obtained from reading this e-book should serve as a starting point for a lifelong dedication to learning, innovation, and taking an active role in the ongoing revolution that Bitcoin is bringing about.

Final thoughts on the potential impact of Bitcoin

Throughout the entirety of this e-book, we have explored the complexities and revolutionary potential of Bitcoin, beginning with its technological underpinnings and progressing through its practical uses and future prospects. In this section, we will present our final thoughts on the possible influence of Bitcoin, taking into consideration its implications for the financial sector, technological advancement, society, and the economy as a whole. We hope to provide a vivid picture of the tremendous influence that Bitcoin is capable of having on the process of building the world in which we live by reflecting on the information that we have acquired and the possibilities that lay ahead of us.

Bitcoin has the potential to transform the current state of the global financial system since it presents an alternative to the established banking systems and to centralized authority. The fact that it is decentralized makes it possible for peer-to-peer transactions, transfers that are not restricted by borders, and increased financial inclusion. Bitcoin's ability to cut out middlemen and lower transaction fees paves the way for unbanked and underbanked populations to gain access to a wider range of financial services.

This, in turn, opens the way for greater economic autonomy for these groups.

The technological advances made by Bitcoin, particularly the blockchain technology that underpins it, have the potential to disrupt a wide variety of businesses in addition to the financial sector. The immutable and transparent characteristic of blockchain technology has the potential to transform established systems and encourage innovation in a variety of domains, including supply chain management, healthcare, voting systems, and intellectual property rights. The foundation of Bitcoin allows for the creation of smart contracts and decentralized applications, which offer limitless possibilities for increasing efficiency, security, and trust.

A decentralized digital currency that enables individuals to gain control over their monetary assets as well as their identities, making it an innovative and valuable asset is known as Bitcoin. Because of its pseudonymous character, it offers a level of secrecy that is not always provided by traditional banking systems. Bitcoin coincides with the ideas of self-sovereign identification and supports privacy rights in a world that is becoming increasingly digital. This is accomplished by providing individuals ownership and control over the personal data that pertains to them.

Bitcoin presents a challenge to the established centralized power structures, not just in the financial industry but outside it as well. Because of the way it is structured, which is decentralized and distributed, it challenges the monopoly that governments and central banks have on the control of monetary policies and financial systems.

Because Bitcoin may enable cross-border transactions without the need for intermediaries, the influence of regulatory barriers is reduced, and it is now possible for financial interactions to occur outside geopolitical boundaries.

In times of economic unpredictability, an asset that has a limited supply and is intrinsically deflationary, like Bitcoin, is likely to be desirable. Bitcoin presents an opportunity for investors seeking a potential hedge against the risks of inflation and devaluation that are associated with traditional fiat currencies. Individuals and institutions have a greater opportunity to preserve their wealth and reduce the negative effects of economic downturns if they diversify their investment portfolios to include Bitcoin.

Bitcoin's potential to reduce barriers to entry into the financial system is one of the most important implications of this decentralized digital currency. Individuals living in underserved locations are able to gain access to the global financial ecosystem through the use of a smartphone and an internet connection. This allows them to take part in economic activities and send and receive value in a safe and effective manner. Bitcoin has the potential to empower previously underserved communities by providing them with access to previously unavailable economic opportunities and removing traditional obstacles to participation.

The significance of Bitcoin extends beyond the boundaries of its own ecosystem. As Bitcoin continues to develop and achieve widespread recognition, it acts as a catalyst for technological improvements in cryptography, cybersecurity, and distributed systems. This is because

Bitcoin functions as a decentralized digital currency. The problems and requirements of Bitcoin contribute to the larger technological landscape, encouraging innovation and molding the future of technology as a whole. This is accomplished through the research and development that is pushed by Bitcoin.

The immutability as well as transparency of the Bitcoin blockchain inspire confidence in the integrity of data and the legitimacy of financial transactions and supply chains. Bitcoin encourages transparency and accountability by doing away with the requirement for third-party middlemen and introducing a ledger that cannot be altered. This enhanced trust has the potential to transform corporate relationships, improve auditing procedures, and produce an atmosphere that is both more efficient and ethical when it comes to conducting commercial transactions and keeping records.

Despite the fact that Bitcoin may have a huge impact in the future, there are still many obstacles and unknowns. There are a number of obstacles that need to be overcome, including regulatory frameworks, worries about scale, concerns about environmental sustainability, and acceptance barriers for users. However, the lessons of history demonstrate that the transformational potential of innovation can frequently transcend initial difficulties, and the ecosystem surrounding Bitcoin continues to adapt and expand.

Bitcoin is a groundbreaking innovation that will affect not only the financial industry but also technology and the way people think about and use money. It has the potential to have a dramatic influence, one that will offer financial empowerment, technical innovation, and a global economy that is more inclusive and transparent. As we come to the end of our exploration of Bitcoin's possibilities, it is essential that we envision a world in which individuals have control over their own financial destinies, innovation is encouraged, and trust is re-established. We can collectively unleash a new era of possibilities and design a world that embraces decentralization, supports innovation, and enables individuals to traverse the digital age with confidence if we comprehend the potential influence that Bitcoin could have and actively participate in its ecosystem.

Thank you for buying and reading/listening to our book. If you found this book useful/helpful please take a few minutes and leave a review on the platform where you purchased our book. Your feedback matters greatly to us.